FOUNDATIONS IN GRACE

A STUDY OF TITUS 2:11-14

GRACE THEOLOGY PRESS

KENNETH R. HODGES

Foundations In Grace
A Study of Titus 2:11-14

Copyright © 2024 by Kenneth R. Hodges
Published by Grace Theology Press.

ISBN: 978-1-63296-703-9
eISBN: 978-1-63296-664-3

TABLE OF CONTENTS

PREFACE

In 2005, shortly after I moved into the role of senior pastor at Emmanuel Baptist Church in Starkville, Mississippi, I undertook the task to write a 16-week Sunday School series that covered the basics of grace. I chose Titus 2:11-14 as the text to launch the study. As I walked through the study with my congregation, it became clear that each component of the outline had further depth that could be explored. This book is that deeper dive. I am ever grateful to the dear saints at Emmanuel who went through the course, offered helpful feedback, and asked good questions that encouraged me to pursue this book.

My prayer for the readers of this book is 1 Timothy 1:5,

But the goal of our instruction is love from a pure heart and a good conscience and a sincere faith.

ACKNOWLEDGMENTS

I thank Dr. Hilton (Butch) Simmons who read each of the original lessons and offered helpful insight. I could not have completed this task without the careful reading and editing of Sam Newton, Kevin Harris, and Holly Harris. Thank you for your discerning eyes and helpful comments. Thanks to Dr. Jim (Nap) Clark who taught me so much about the grace of God. I am grateful for Dr. Dave Anderson and Dr. Fred Chay, both friends and mentors at Grace School of Theology. Special thanks to the congregation of Emmanuel Baptist Church, Starkville, MS, many of whom went through this series as a Sunday School class. Of course, this project would not be possible without the faithful monetary support of so many – thank you! Most of all, I want to thank my family, Kaye, Holly & Kevin, and Joe Warner for their encouragement and prayers.

DEDICATION

To all those saints who wish to grow deeper in their understanding of God's marvelous grace! May you build on the foundation of Jesus Christ with gold, silver, and precious stones. Artist MaryEsther Elam captured the idea beautifully:

You also, as living stones, are being built up as a spiritual house for a holy priesthood, to offer up spiritual sacrifices acceptable to God through Jesus Christ. (1 Pet 2:5)

Be diligent to present yourself approved to God as a workman who does not need to be ashamed, accurately handling the word of truth. (2 Tim 2:15)

For no man can lay a foundation other than the one which is laid, which is Jesus Christ. (1 Cor 3:11)

FOREWORD

Wise is the parent who can distinguish the difference between ACCEPTANCE and APPROVAL as it pertains to their children. Many children have the impression that they have to perform in order to win their parents' love. Such children often view their father as a harsh disciplinarian who is constantly pointing out what they get wrong and seldom catching them doing something right. Children in homes like this seldom find much joy. But the parents who can communicate 100% unconditional love for their children regardless of their performance actually find their children living up to their potential more consistently than those children who are performing to earn their parents' love.

Now there is nothing wrong with wanting our children to perform well. However, how they perform should only affect our APPROVAL, not our ACCEPTANCE. If my child becomes a drug addict and never holds a job, he still has my ACCEPTANCE but does not have my APPROVAL. Dr. Hodges shows us how these same distinctions between ACCEPTANCE and APPROVAL apply to our relationship with God. Every child who enters the family of God has His ACCEPTANCE. Spiritual birth through faith in Jesus Christ without any meritorious works ushers a person into the family of God. But that is just the beginning of a spiritual life with our heavenly Father that can get better and better as we learn to love Him by keeping His commandments and enjoy His APPROVAL.

So often spiritual teachers tell us we must perform (keep God's commandments) in order to win His love (ACCEPTANCE). Those who adhere to that kind of teaching will always live in fear of not behaving well enough to get God's ACCEPTANCE. Dr. Hodges makes a clear distinction between God's ACCEPTANCE and God's APPROVAL. The former comes through believing in Christ (ACCEPTANCE) while the latter comes through obedience (APPROVAL). We receive our ACCEPTANCE while we are alive on earth, but we receive our APPROVAL at the Judgment Seat of Christ in the next life.

Dr. Hodges clarifies all this through explaining the difference between justification and sanctification. He wants us to understand that justification is for ACCEPTANCE while sanctification is for APPROVAL. Too many attach the requirements for sanctification to the requirements for justification. In doing so, they not only muddy the gospel waters, but they also turn living for Christ into a "have-to" life instead of a "thank you" life. The former turns living a godly life into a job, while the latter turns the same into a joy. Dr. Hodges does a marvelous job of showing us how the free grace of God does not promote license to live an ungodly life but love to live a godly life. He uses Titus 2:11-14 as the foundation for his entire book. That's where God uses His grace to "teach" us to become godly.

One of Dr. Hodges' gifts is to bring the big theological concepts (redemption, propitiation, atonement, etc.) out of the clouds onto the coffee table. Anyone can complicate, but not everyone can simplify. I hope Dr. Hodges' clear and simple explanations will help every reader to better sort out and enjoy the eternal truths—how we can maximize our life with Him while we are on earth so that we can magnify His glory when we are with Him in heaven.

Dr. David R. Anderson
Founder and President, Grace School of Theology
Author, *Free Grace Soteriology*

For the grace of God...

INTRODUCTION

Grace! We say it over our meals. We use the word as an adjective to describe certain people. We sing about grace. We use the word grace to name our children. I even have a Boston Terrier that I named Gracie! Because we use the word grace in so many ways, it only makes sense that, in order to begin a study called *Foundations in Grace*, we should define and understand the biblical uses of this word. Charles Swindoll, popular author and founder of "Insight for Living,"[1] points out, "The Bible never gives us a one-statement definition, though grace appears throughout its pages..."[2] Charles Ryrie, author of the *Ryrie Study Bible*, writes, "Christianity is distinct from all other religions because it is a message of grace. Jesus Christ is the supreme revelation of God's grace; salvation is by grace; and grace governs and empowers Christian living. Without grace Christianity is nothing."[3] J. F. Strombeck, a successful toy manufacturer in the early twentieth century, wrote a series of books on grace. In his book *So Great Salvation*, he writes,

---

1 https://insight.org/
2 Charles R. Swindoll, *The Grace Awakening* (Dallas: Word Publishing, 1990), 8.
3 Charles C. Ryrie, *The Grace of God* (Chicago: Moody Press, 1975), 9.

"Grace is one of the greatest words in the Bible. It speaks not of what man does for God but what God does for man."[4] On the importance of grace, Charles Bing, author of *Simply By Grace* and founder of GraceLife Ministries, writes, "…one's concept of God's grace is not only the key to becoming a Christian, but it is also the key to the assurance of salvation and living in freedom to serve God and others."[5] The importance of understanding grace cannot be overstated!

To understand the concept of grace as it is revealed in the Bible, we need to start with a brief study of the words used. Ryrie states, "Word studies are a must if one is to have a full and correct understanding of grace… A proper concept is built on facts. So the facts about grace must be understood before the concept is formed…"[6] While the Old Testament is full of demonstrations of the grace of God toward his people, the concept of grace, as we see it more fully developed in the New Testament, is not as clearly evident in the Old Testament. Because of this, the Old Testament is sometimes misunderstood, or perhaps we could say, the God of the Old Testament is misunderstood. One early church theologian, Marcion of Sinope, preached that the God of the Old Testament, Yahweh, was belligerent, vindictive, and vengeful, and sought to punish mankind. Marcion thought the God of the New Testament, Jesus, was gracious and loving and sought to save mankind. In essence, he denied "that the God of the Jewish Scriptures (for Christians, the Old Testament) was the same as the God of Christian Scriptures."[7] Of course, his teachings were deemed heretical by the early church fathers. However, for some, there still exists an uneasy feeling about the Old Testament portrayal of God. Was God less gracious in the Old Testament? If we are to understand the nature of God's grace in the Old Testament, we must get back to our word studies.

---

4 J. F. Strombeck, *So Great Salvation* (Moline, Ill., Strombeck Agency, Inc. 1947), 108.
5 Charles C. Bing, *Simply by Grace* (Grand Rapids: Kregel Publications, 2009), 12.
6 Ryrie, *The Grace of God*, 10.
7 Charles J. Schmidt, "Marcion," ed. John D. Barry et al., *The Lexham Bible Dictionary* (Bellingham, WA: Lexham Press, 2016).

There are two main words in the Old Testament that convey the idea of God's grace. The first is *chen* which is defined as, *"to yearn towards, long for, be merciful, compassionate, favorable, to be inclined towards."*[8] Numbers 6:24-25 says, *"The LORD bless you, and keep you; the LORD make His face shine on you, and be gracious to you."* The Psalmist often cried to God for His grace:

Be gracious to me, O LORD, for I am pining away... (Ps 6:2)

Turn to me and be gracious to me, For I am lonely and afflicted. (Ps 25:16)

Thirty times in the Psalms alone the word *chen* is used speaking of God's gracious favor. *Chen* relates the idea of a superior (God) who bestows unmerited favor to those who are inferior (mankind). While most of the usages of *chen* speak of temporal favor, a few do connect the idea of redemption with God's gracious favor. For example, in Psalm 26:11 David says, *"But as for me, I shall walk in my integrity; redeem me, and be gracious to me."* Ryrie summarizes, "At best it can only be said that this doctrinal relationship between redemption and *chen*, grace, is but scantily revealed in the Old Testament."[9] Nevertheless, we do begin to get a glimpse of God's gracious nature as he pours out his love and favor on those who seek Him, even though they are undeserving.

The second Old Testament word that is related to the New Testament concept of grace is *chesed* which occurs 245 times in the Old Testament. When speaking of God, *chesed* is defined as, *"kindness, lovingkindness* in condescending to the needs of his creatures."[10] Ryrie observes, "...*chesed* involves a relationship between those involved in the act of kindness performed... So important is this idea of relationship

---

8 Brown, Driver, Briggs, *Hebrew and English Lexicon,* 335.

9 Ryrie, *The Grace of God,* 15.

10 Brown, Driver, Briggs, *Hebrew and English Lexicon,* 339.

in *chesed* that it may be said that *chesed* becomes the basis on which the relationship exists and grows."[11] This relational aspect of *chesed* stresses God's faithfulness in the relationship. We might define *chesed* as God's kindness and mercy demonstrated through his steadfast faithfulness. *Chesed* is often expressed in the covenant relationships God has with Israel. Note the Word of God delivered by Nathan the prophet concerning the Davidic Covenant in 2 Samuel 7:13-17:

> *He shall build a house for My name, and I will establish the throne of his kingdom forever. I will be a father to him and he will be a son to Me; when he commits iniquity, I will correct him with the rod of men and the strokes of the sons of men, but My lovingkindness (chesed) shall not depart from him, as I took it away from Saul, whom I removed from before you. Your house and your kingdom shall endure before Me forever; your throne shall be established forever. In accordance with all these words and all this vision, so Nathan spoke to David.*

Indeed, praise, forgiveness, deliverance, and protection are all connected to God's *chesed*.

Summarizing these two Old Testament words, Ryrie writes,

> *Chen* is the unmerited favor of a superior to an inferior, which in the case of God as superior is expressed to man usually in temporal and occasionally in spiritual blessings and in deliverance in both physical and spiritual senses.

> *Chesed* is the firm loving-kindness expressed between related people and particularly in the covenants into which God entered with His people and which His *chesed* firmly guaranteed.[12]

---

11 Ryrie, *The Grace of God*, 16.
12 Ibid., 20.

So we see God in the Old Testament bestowing His undeserved blessings both physically and spiritually upon those who are in a loving relationship with Him. However, it is in the New Testament that we come to know the full meaning of God's grace. As we shall see, it is the appearing of Jesus Christ in human history that is the ultimate expression of grace. But let's first look at the New Testament word.

The Greek word translated as "grace" in the New Testament is the word *charis*. However, before the New Testament, there was another version of the Greek Bible written. Because Israel was in captivity in a Greek-speaking culture, the Old Testament was translated into Greek. This Greek version of the Old Testament is called the Septuagint, which is abbreviated as LXX. "The term Septuagint, meaning "seventy," actually refers to the seventy-two translators—six from each tribe of Israel—involved in translating the Pentateuch from Hebrew to Greek in the third-century BCE (seventy-two is rounded down to seventy, hence the Roman numeral LXX)."[13] In the Septuagint, we find the Hebrew word *chen* translated by the Greek word *charis* 61 times. *Chesed* is only translated with *charis* two times (Esther 2:9, 17). *Chesed* is most often translated by another Greek word, *eleos,* which means, "...to show kindness or concern for someone in serious need—to show mercy, to be merciful toward, to have mercy on, mercy."[14] Nevertheless, we see in the LXX the roots of the New Testament meaning of grace, *charis*, beginning to take shape. The Greek lexicons give the following meanings for *charis*:

1. "To show kindness to someone, with the implication of graciousness on the part of the one showing such kindness..."[15]
2. "Good will, favor. Conveys the sense of a gift of kindness and favor given to a person or persons..."[16]

---

13 https://www.thegospelcoalition.org/article/what-is-the-septuagint/

14 Johannes P. Louw and Eugene Albert Nida, *Greek-English Lexicon of the New Testament: Based on Semantic Domains* (New York: United Bible Societies, 1996), 750.

15 Ibid., 748.

16 Joshua G. Mathews, "Blessing," ed. Douglas Mangum et al., *Lexham Theological Wordbook*, Lexham Bible Reference Series (Bellingham, WA: Lexham Press, 2014).

This basic definition is broken down into several categories of usage in the New Testament. One Greek-English Lexicon lists the following five nuances:

1. "A winning quality or attractiveness that invites a favorable reaction..."[17]

   Luke 4:22 would be an example of this usage, *"And all were speaking well of Him, and wondering at the gracious words which were falling from His lips; and they were saying, "Is this not Joseph's son?"* Gracious speech is also mentioned by the Apostle Paul in Colossians 4:6, *"Let your speech always be with grace, as though seasoned with salt, so that you will know how you should respond to each person."*

2. "A beneficent disposition toward someone..."[18]

   We often see this in relation to the grace of God. Romans 3:24 is an example, *"Being justified as a gift by His grace through the redemption which is in Christ Jesus."* Paul writes in 2 Timothy 1:9, *"...who has saved us and called us with a holy calling, not according to our works, but according to His own purpose and grace which was granted us in Christ Jesus from all eternity."*

3. "A practical application of goodwill..."[19]

   We often see this usage in the phrase *the grace of God or the grace of Christ.* Examples would be Hebrews 12:15, *"See to it that no one comes short of the grace of God; that no root of bitterness springing up causes trouble, and by it*

---

17 William Arndt, Frederick W. Danker, et al., *A Greek-English Lexicon of the New Testament and Other Early Christian Literature* (Chicago: University of Chicago Press, 2000), 1079.

18 Ibid., 1079.

19 Ibid.

many be defiled" and 2 Timothy 2:1, *"You therefore, my son, be strong in the grace that is in Christ Jesus."*

4. "An exceptional effect produced by generosity..."[20]

    Note Paul's words in 1 Corinthians 15:10, *"But by the grace of God I am what I am, and His grace toward me did not prove vain; but I labored even more than all of them, yet not I, but the grace of God with me."* Notice the effect of grace on Stephen in Acts 6:8, *"And Stephen, full of grace and power, was performing great wonders and signs among the people."*

5. "A response to generosity or beneficence, *thanks, gratitude...*"[21]

    In this usage, *charis* is often translated by the word *thanks*. For example, 2 Corinthians 9:15, *"Thanks (charis) be to God for His indescribable gift!"*

In relation to God, Bing boils all of these usages of the word *charis* into a simple thought, "Grace is God's loving way of meeting our needs by showing us favor we do not deserve."[22] The highest demonstration of God's grace is in the person of His Son, Jesus Christ. Ryrie adds, "... grace is the favor of God in giving His Son and the benefit to men of receiving that Son."[23] Ryrie continues, "The lavish gift of God in the person of His Son is the particularly New Testament meaning of grace. This is why it is quite true to say that *charis* is a word that has been raised to higher level and filled with new meaning by our Lord Jesus Christ. His self-sacrifice is grace itself..."[24] John 1:16-17 states, *"For of His fullness we have all received, and grace upon grace. For the Law was*

---

20 William Arndt, Frederick W. Danker, et al., *A Greek-English Lexicon*, 1079.
21 Ibid.
22 Bing, *Simply by Grace*, 17.
23 Ryrie, *The Grace of God*, 24.
24 Ibid., 25.

given through Moses; grace and truth were realized through Jesus Christ."
A few verses later in John 1:29, John writes, *"Behold the Lamb of God
who takes away the sin of the world!"* It is in the appearing and ministry
of Jesus Christ that we see grace most beautifully explained. His death
on the cross as the complete, final payment for sin is offered to all on the
basis of God's grace. Paul writes to the believers in Ephesus in Ephesians
2:8-9, *"For by grace you have been saved through faith; and that not of
yourselves, it is the gift of God; not as a result of works, so that no one may
boast."* We clearly see a couple of things about eternal salvation in these
verses. First, it is by God's grace; He is the one who makes the provision.
Second, this salvation is a *gift*! These two concepts are also seen clearly
in Romans 3:23-24, *"For all have sinned and fall short of the glory of God,
being justified as a gift by His grace through the redemption which is in
Christ Jesus."* Our justification (salvation) is a gift, and it is by God's
grace! As a matter of fact, three times in Romans Paul uses a form of
charis that is translated "free gift" (Rom 5:15-16 and 6:23). Romans 6:23
states, *"For the wages of sin is death, but the free gift (charisma) of God
is eternal life in Christ Jesus our Lord."* David Anderson, president of
Grace School of Theology and, author of *Free Grace Soteriology*, writes,
"Paul qualifies grace by saying it is a free gift. A free gift has no strings
attached on the front end (or it becomes a wage) and no strings attached
on the back end (or it is a bribe)."[25]

Grace truly is amazing! The English acronym for G.R.A.C.E., God's
Riches At Christ's Expense, is accurate. Songwriter Phil Wickham in his
song, "This Is Amazing Grace," pens these lyrics:

> This is amazing grace, this is unfailing love
> That You would take my place, that You would bear my cross
> You laid down Your life, that I would be set free Oh, Jesus,
> I sing for, all that You've done for me[26]

---

25 David R. Anderson, *Free Grace Theology*, 3rd ed. (The Woodlands, TX: Grace Theology
Press, 2018), x.

26 https://www.azlyrics.com/lyrics/philwickham/thisisamazinggrace.html

In Acts 20:24, Paul calls this good news about Jesus Christ "the gospel of the grace of God." Grace truly is good news! It is God's underserved favor! However, there is a difference between grace and mercy. Mercy is *not getting* what we deserve. Grace is getting what we *do not deserve.*

In 2000, I had the privilege of traveling to Russia to minister to Russian youth at summer camps. Of course, we purchased the cheapest airline tickets we could, trying to make the trip as affordable as possible. As we were about to board to return home to the USA, the ticket official informed us that there were not enough seats in coach class where we had our tickets, thus some members of our team would be bumped to first class. He then read four or five names of people from our group. Mine was not one of the names! For those of us who did not hear our name called, we enjoyed the flight home in the seats we had purchased. For those who did hear their names called, they flew home in style in the first-class section. This is an illustration of grace, as those who were bumped to first class did not deserve it because they had not paid for it, nor had they done anything to merit it. It was a free gift! Our sin has purchased us death, both physical and eternal. However, God loved us so much that by His grace, he provided the payment for our sin in the person of His Son, Jesus. We can't earn it, as it is a gift. We simply must receive it. The price is paid, the gift is offered, but we must believe in Jesus to receive the gift of eternal life. The words *believe* and *faith* are from the same Greek word and basically mean that we take God at His word. Understanding God's grace and His offer of life in His Son as a gift is to understand the gospel of grace.

For the grace of God Has appeared…

CHAPTER 1:
THE PERSON OF CHRIST

We saw that the ultimate picture of God's grace is the Lord Jesus Christ. But who is this person? How do we know if He was truly the Son of God, the promised Messiah of Israel? Were His miracles and teachings simply revisionist history added by a group of men who wanted to make Him a savior? Is there a way, from the Bible, that we can settle the question Jesus asked his disciples, "Who do you say that I am?"[1] Understanding the person and work of Jesus is a crucial step to developing a strong, grounded faith and walk with Him. In this chapter, we will look at the person of Christ. We will first look at the promises and prophecies of Scripture that pinpoint the time, place, and manner of His birth, and then the Scriptures that establish His deity.

When I was growing up, my mother—when speaking of someone who she thought was off on their viewpoint—used to say, "He can't see

---

1 Matthew 16:15

the forest for the trees!" The same is true in any Bible study: context is king! It is important to step back and get the big picture before we look at the details. Theologians call the big picture of the Bible the metanarrative. A metanarrative is defined as, "...the 'big picture' or all-encompassing theme that unites all smaller themes and individual stories."[2] Some think that the church is the big story of the Bible but, as important as the church is, she is not the big story. Others say that Israel is the big story, but Israel is also just a piece of the big story. Many theologians insist that the redemption of mankind is the metanarrative of the Bible. Redemption is a major story line that runs through the Bible, but I would suggest that there is an even bigger story or metanarrative. As one author puts it, "From Genesis to Revelation, the Bible is telling us about the reign and rule of God. This is the Big Story of the Bible, the purpose for which it was written. Each of its sixty-six books contributes to telling this Big Story—a story of creation, fall, redemption, and restoration. The Bible purposes to tell us this Big Story in a thousand smaller stories, from its first page to its last."[3] So the metanarrative of the Bible is actually the glory of God. God, in His divine wisdom, sovereignty, omniscience, foreknowledge, along with all His divine attributes, determined to create mankind in His own image. However, the creation of man was not God's first creative act. The Bible makes it clear that there is a heavenly host of beings, angels and others, that God created and brought into His presence. Some theologians call this heavenly host God's *divine counsel.* They are an "...assembly of divine beings who administer the affairs of the cosmos under Yahweh, the God of Israel."[4] God asks Job, "Where were you at My laying the foundation of the earth... when the morning stars were singing together and all

---

2 https://www.gotquestions.org/metanarrative.html

3 https://www.biblestudytools.com/bible-study/topical-studies/study-with-purpose-seeing-the-big-story-of-the-bible.html

4 Michael S. Heiser, "Divine Council," ed. John D. Barry et al., *The Lexham Bible Dictionary* (Bellingham, WA: Lexham Press, 2016.)

the sons of God shouted for joy?"[5] The point is, God had a plan for the creation of the earth and mankind, and the heavenly host rejoiced to see Him bring it about. It is clear that at some point after the creation of the heavenly host, sin entered the universe and Satan and a number of the angels rebelled against God. Most theologians believe that Isaiah 14:12-14 and Ezekiel 28:12-18 describe this event. Against the backdrop of this heavenly rebellion, God still decided to create man in His image and place him over the earth. However, that plan was damaged by the fall of Adam and Eve in Genesis 3. Clearly God, in his foreknowledge and omniscience, knew that man would fall, but he did not determine that man would fall. Adam and Eve had a real choice to respond properly to God's commands. This tension between God's sovereignty and man's responsibility has been a theological debate for centuries, but God did not create robots that had no choice. God foreknew the fall but did not predetermine it. God also had a plan for the rescue of mankind based on His foreknowledge and omniscience. He would send his own Son, Jesus, to pay the price for man's sin and open the door for restored relationship and fellowship. The plan begins in Genesis 3 and flows through the Old Testament, becoming more and more specific as revelation progresses. I call these 'road signs to the Messiah'. Let's look at a few of these signs.

1. The Promised Seed — In Genesis 3:14-15, God tells the serpent (Satan) that there will be one born of Eve's lineage that will "bruise him on the head," speaking of a death blow to his plan and rebellion. This death blow was delivered when Jesus died on the cross and defeated the power of death. However, there will be a struggle as the heel of the "seed" will be bruised.

2. The line of Seth — Eve had two sons: Cain and Abel. Cain was the firstborn, and it is probable that Eve believed Cain would be the "seed" that was promised. However, Cain murders Able and in Genesis 4:25, we are told that God gives Adam and Eve another son, Seth, through whom the promised seed

---

5 Job 38:4-7

will come. The struggle between Satan and the lineage of the seed is ongoing as in Genesis 6, Satan attempts to corrupt the human race and destroy the godly line. This brings about the flood through which Noah, who is a descendant of Seth, and his family are the only humans saved through the ark. Noah has three sons: Shem, Ham, and Japheth.

3. The blessings on Shem — We see the events of the flood in Genesis 7 through 9 and then in Chapters 10 and 11 the genealogies of Japheth, Ham, and Shem. In the middle of this record is the account of the Tower of Babel where God confuses the language of men so that they cannot understand one another, and God scatters them on the face of the earth. In Genesis chapter 11, we find the descendants of Shem and the genealogy concludes with Terah who had three sons, Abram, Nahor, and Haran.

4. The call of Abram — Of Terah's three sons, it is Abram that God calls in Genesis 12:1-3. Abram is given three wonderful promises: 1) The seed will come out of a specific land, 2) The seed will come from a specific nation, and 3) The seed will be a blessing for all the nations.

5. Isaac — God establishes a covenant with Abram in Genesis 17, and it is here that Abram's name, which means "exalted father," is changed to Abraham, which means "the father of a great number." Of course, in Genesis 16, Sarai and Abram, trying to help God, arranged for Abraham to have a son by Sarai's maid, Hagar, whom they named Ishmael. But it was not to be the linage of Ishmael through which the seed would come. In Genesis 17:16, God promises Abraham a son by Sarah and in 17:19, God promises that He will establish the covenant with this son. That son, born to Abraham and Sarah in their old age, is Isaac.

6. Jacob — Isaac marries Rebekah, and the Lord blesses them with twins, Esau and Jacob. However, in Genesis 25:22-23, the Lord chooses the younger, Jacob, to be the lineage of the seed.

7. The Tribe of Judah — In Genesis 49, Jacob blesses his twelve sons. Verses 8-12 document the blessings to Judah. The name Judah means "praise." God is going to do something through the Tribe of Judah that will cause men to lift their voices in praise to the coming seed. Verse 10 promises that *"The scepter shall not depart from Judah, nor the ruler's staff from between his feet, until Shiloh comes, and to him shall be the obedience of the peoples."* The "scepter" refers to the right to rule or reign. Shiloh, which means peaceful or peacemaker, is a Messianic title for the "seed" who will also be a deliverer.

8. The Family of Jesse — Within the Tribe of Judah, a specific family is chosen. In 1 Samuel 16:1, the Lord says, *"...Fill your horn with oil, and go; I will send you to Jesse the Bethlehemite, for I have selected a king for Myself among his sons."*

9. David — When Samuel interviews the sons of Jesse, it is the youngest, David, that Samuel anoints. In 1 Samuel 16:12-13, the Lord says, *"Arise, anoint him: for this is he."*

10. The Royal Genealogies — Matthew 1:1-16 gives the royal genealogy of Jesus that begins with Abraham and ends with Joseph, his legal father. Matthew 1:16 is clear that Joseph is the husband of Mary, but it is through Mary that Jesus is born. Of course, Mary is also of part of the royal genealogy and her lineage is given in Luke 3:23-38 where it begins with Joseph (the legal father) and goes all the way back to Adam who was the son of God.

11. The Time of Birth — From Daniel 9:24-27, the time of the birth of the *seed*, the Messiah, can be calculated to within a few months. Four hundred and ninety years (70 sevens of years) are prophesized for the completion of Israel's history from the time of the issuing of a decree to restore and rebuild Jerusalem. We can document the decree of Artaxerxes Longimanus as being given in 445 B.C. (Neh 2:6-9). The Seventy Weeks are divided into seven weeks (49 years), plus 62 weeks (434 years), plus a final one week (7 years). It is after the first 69 weeks, or

483 years, that Daniel tells us the Messiah will be "cut off." This is a reference to the crucifixion of Jesus which occurred in 33 A.D., which is exactly the time Daniel predicted centuries earlier. Artaxerxes' decree in 445 B.C. plus 483 years comes out to be 33 A.D. We know Jesus was in His early thirties at the time of His death, so His birth can be established to within a few months.

12. The Virgin Birth — Isaiah 7:14, *"Therefore the Lord Himself will give you a sign; Behold, a virgin will be with child and bear a son, and she will call His name Immanuel."* The word for virgin here refers to a chaste maiden who is unmarried. However, there is something about this birth that will be a sign. The New Testament clarifies the supernatural understanding in Matthew 1:18-25 where Isaiah 7:14 is quoted and Mary is said to be kept a virgin until she gave birth to Jesus, the promised seed.

13. The place of birth — Micah 5:2, *"But as for you, Bethlehem Ephrathah, too little to be among the clans of Judah, from you One will go forth for Me to be ruler in Israel. His goings forth are from long ago, from the days of eternity."* Joseph and Mary lived in Nazareth but had to go to Bethlehem for a census, because they were of the house and family of David. In fulfilment of the prophecy, Mary gave birth to Jesus in Bethlehem (Lk 2:4-7).

14. The forerunner, John the Baptist — In Malachi 3:1, the Lord proclaims, *"Behold, I am going to send My messenger, and he will clear the way before Me. And the Lord, whom you seek, will suddenly come to His temple; and the messenger of the covenant, in whom you delight, behold, He is coming..."* A similar prophecy is given in Isaiah 40:3. Matthew 3:1-3 states, *"Now in those days John the Baptist came, preaching in the wilderness of Judea, saying, 'Repent, for the kingdom of heaven is at hand.' For this is the one referred to by Isaiah the prophet when he said, 'The voice of one crying in the wilderness, make ready the way of the Lord, make His paths straight.'"* While John is in the womb of

Elizabeth, he leaps when he hears the voice of Mary because he can feel the presence of the baby Jesus in Mary's womb.

15. The Divine Announcement — Luke 2:9-11, *"And an angel of the Lord suddenly stood before them, and the glory of the Lord shone around them; and they were terribly frightened. But the angel said to them, "Do not be afraid; for behold, I bring you good news of great joy which will be for all the people; for today in the city of David there has been born for you a Savior, who is Christ the Lord."*

16. Fulfilled Prophecy — The gospels are full of prophecies that were fulfilled by Jesus. Mathematician Peter Stoner wrote a book in 1944 entitled *Science Speaks*[6] in which he used the well-known principle of probability to establish how incredibly accurate the Bible is prophetically and how it would be impossible for certain events to be randomly fulfilled. Stoner used only eight prophecies that Jesus fulfilled and found the probability of chance fulfillment to be 1 in 10^{17}. That's one in one hundred quadrillion! Stoner gives an illustration to help us understand the magnitude of this number:

Suppose that we take 10^{17} silver dollars and lay them on the face of Texas. They will cover all of the state two feet deep. Now mark one of these silver dollars and stir the whole mass thoroughly, all over the state. Blindfold a man and tell him that he can travel as far as he wishes, but he must pick up one silver dollar and say that this is the right one. What chance would he have of getting the right one? Just the same chance that the prophets would have had of writing these eight prophecies and having them all come true in any one man, from their day to the present time, providing they wrote using their own wisdom.[7]

---

6 https://archive.org/details/sciencespeakspeterw.stoner/mode/2up. Although Stoner's book is out of print, the entire book is available online at this site.

7 Ibid., 63.

Jesus, in his birth, life, death, and resurrection, fulfilled over 300 Old Testament prophecies, 108 of these being Messianic prophecies. Calculating just 48, the odds increase to 1 in 10^{157}. Stoner states, "The bottom line is that the fulfillment of Bible prophecy in the life of Jesus proves conclusively that He truly was God in the flesh."[8] It also proves the supernatural origin of the Bible. He summarizes, "Any man who rejects Christ as the Son of God is rejecting a fact proved perhaps more absolutely than any other fact in the world."[9]

Putting all the above together, it is clear that Jesus was the promised seed of Genesis 3:15. But who is this seed? Was Jesus God in the flesh or simply a very special man that God granted many supernatural powers? It is clear that Christ was human as He possessed a human body, soul, and spirit. He was Jewish and was recognized as such. Even though God was His Father, Jesus did have a human mother. He developed just like other humans. Luke 2:40 states, *"And the Child continued to grow and become strong, increasing in wisdom; and the grace of God was upon Him."* It is also clear that Jesus did not sin in his humanity. Jesus was the only perfect human being the world has ever seen. He did not have a sin nature and never sinned. In 2 Corinthians 5:21, Paul writes, *"He made Him who knew no sin to be sin on our behalf, that we might become the righteousness of God in Him."*

When we speak of the deity of Christ, we are speaking of His divine nature, or simply stating that Jesus is God. There are a number of ways that the Bible presents Christ in His deity. Below are a few examples in four areas:

1. Divine predictions — An example would be Isaiah 9:6, *"For a child will be born to us, a son will be given to us; And the government will rest on His shoulders; And His name will be called Wonderful Counselor, Mighty God, Eternal Father, Prince of Peace."* Notice that the child is born, that is, in his humanity

---

8 https://archive.org/details/sciencespeakspeterw.stoner/mode/2up, p64.
9 Ibid., 66.

he had a birth, but that the Son is given. His sonship is eternal. This is a Messianic prophecy as the government will rest on His shoulders during the millennial kingdom. Two of the names by which He will be called are *Mighty God* and *Eternal Father*!

2. Divine names — Jesus is called God often in the Bible. Some examples are as follows: John 20:28 where Thomas says, "*My Lord and my God!*"; 1 John 5:20, "*And we know that the Son of God has come, and has given us understanding, in order that we might know Him who is true, and we are in Him who is true, in His Son Jesus Christ. This is the true God and eternal life.*"; Revelation 19:16, "*And on His robe and on His thigh He has a name written, "KING OF KINGS, AND LORD OF LORDS.*"; Revelation 1:17, "*And when I saw Him, I fell at His feet as a dead man. And He laid His right hand upon me, saying, "Do not be afraid; I am the first and the last."* A few verses earlier in Revelation 1:8, God the Father is called the Alpha and the Omega, a parallel phrase.

3. Divine Equality and Worship — In Isaiah 42:8, God states, "*I am the LORD, that is My name; I will not give My glory to another, Nor My praise to graven images.*" Clearly, God will not share his glory with anyone, yet Christ did share God's glory, meaning He was one in essence with the Father. Some examples are as follows: John 17:5, "*And now, glorify Thou Me together with Thyself, Father, with the glory which I had with Thee before the world was.*"; Colossians 2:9, "*For in Him all the fullness of Deity dwells in bodily form.*"; Philippians 2:6, "*who, although He existed in the form of God, did not regard equality with God a thing to be grasped.*"; John 10:30, "*I and the Father are one.*"; Hebrews 1:6, "*And when He again brings the first-born into the world, He says, 'AND LET ALL THE ANGELS OF GOD WORSHIP HIM.'*" The Lord proclaims in Isaiah 43:10b-11, "*Before Me there was no God formed, and there will be none after Me. I, even I, am the LORD; and there is no savior besides*

ME." However, in Titus 2:13, Jesus is called *"...our great God and Savior..."* In Zechariah 12:4-10, it is the LORD (Yahweh) who is speaking and He says, *"...they will look on Me whom they have pierced; and they will mourn for Him, as one mourns for an only son, and they will weep bitterly over Him, like the bitter weeping over a firstborn."* In Isaiah 53:5, which speaks of the coming Messiah, Jesus, the prophet says, *"But He was pierced through for our transgressions, He was crushed for our iniquities; the chastening for our well-being fell upon Him, and by His scourging we are healed."*

4. Divine attributes — Many of God's divine attributes are seen in Jesus.

   a. Omnipotence (All powerful)

   "And Jesus came up and spoke to them, saying, 'All authority has been given to Me in heaven and on earth.'" (Matt 28:18)

   "For by Him all things were created, both in the heavens and on earth, visible and invisible, whether thrones or dominions or rulers or authorities - all things have been created by Him and for Him. And He is before all things, and in Him all things hold together." (Col 1:16-17)

   b. Omniscience (All knowing)

   "Now we know that You know all things, and have no need for anyone to question You; by this we believe that You came from God." (Jn 16:30)

   c. Omnipresent (Always present)

   "...teaching them to observe all that I commanded you; and lo, I am with you always, even to the end of the age." (Matt 28:20)

d. Immutability (Never changing)

> "…but He, on the other hand, because He abides forever, holds His priesthood permanently." (Heb 7:24)

> "Jesus Christ is the same yesterday and today, yes and forever." (Heb 13:8)

e. Everlastingness

> "Jesus said to them, "Truly, truly, I say to you, before Abraham was born, I am." (Jn 8:58)

f. Holiness

> "And you know that He appeared in order to take away sins; and in Him there is no sin." (1 Jn 3:5)

> "WHO COMMITTED NO SIN, NOR WAS ANY DECEIT FOUND IN HIS MOUTH." (1 Pet 2:22)

g. Love

> "…and to know the love of Christ which surpasses knowledge, that you may be filled up to all the fullness of God." (Eph 3:19)

Understanding how the God of the universe could take on human flesh and live among us is truly mind boggling, yet the Bible declares this to be true. Christ was not simply God and Man—He was the GOD-MAN. Two natures with one personality. As Paul proclaimed, "The grace of God has appeared!"

Bringing salvation…

CHAPTER 2:

THE GOSPEL

When most people hear the word salvation, they assume that it is speaking of our eternal salvation. However, of the approximate 46 uses of the noun *salvation* and the 107 uses of the verb *saved*, over half are not referring to eternal salvation. The noun salvation (*soteria*) is defined as deliverance and the verb (*sozo*) as to save or deliver. The question must always be asked, "Deliverance from what?" Of course, the context reveals the answer. In Matthew 8:25, when the disciples cried out, *"Save us, Lord; we are perishing,"* we must remember the context. They are in a boat on the Sea of Galilee in the middle of a great storm and the boat is about to sink. They are crying out for physical deliverance from drowning. An often misinterpreted verse is Matthew 24:13 where Jesus states, *"But the one who endures to the end, he will be saved."* This is not talking about enduring to the end of your life in order to go to heaven. The context of Matthew 24 is the tribulation. A few verses later in verse 22, Jesus says, *"Unless those days had been cut short, no life would have been saved; but for the sake of the elect those days will be cut short."* The salvation, or deliverance spoken about in these verses is physical deliverance. It is wise to always determine, from the context, from what one is being saved. The following chart helps distinguish between the three phases of salvation:

JUSTIFICATION	SANCTIFICATION	GLORIFICATION
Our *Position* in Christ	Our *Condition* in This World	Our *State* in Heaven
Saved from the *penalty* of sin Romans 5:1	Saved from the *power* of sin Romans 6-8	Saved from the *presence* of sin 1 Peter 1:3-5
Happens the moment we believe Romans 4:5, John 6:47, Ephesians 1:13	Happens over the course of our lives Ephesians 4:1, 2 Timothy 2:15, 1 Peter 2:2	Happens at death or the Rapture 1 Thessalonians 4:15-17
We are *declared righteous* 2 Corinthians 5:21	We are *becoming righteous*, growing in Christlikeness Galatians 5:16, Colossians 3:2-3	We *are righteous* Philippians 3:20-21

If we confuse sanctification truth with justification truth, the results will be a perverted, works-based gospel.

In Titus 2:11, Paul has in mind God's grace that both saves a person eternally the moment he or she believes, and also saves people temporally as they walk with Him. The word *salvation* in verse 11 is actually an adjective that qualifies *grace*. It is the *salvation bringing grace* that has appeared in the person of Jesus Christ. This grace is said to be for "all men." We will explore the idea of grace offered to all in a later chapter. Here, we want to develop the content of the gospel, the means in which God's grace is presented to mankind. The gospel of the grace of God is the good news about Jesus Christ. It is the proclamation of the person and work of Christ. The word gospel (*euangelion*) means *good news* or *glad tidings*. There are three gospels mentioned in the New Testament: the gospel of the kingdom (Matt 4:23), the gospel of the grace of God (Acts 20:24), and the eternal gospel (Rev 14:6).

The gospel of the kingdom was the good news that the King was present and the promised kingdom for Israel was being offered, that is, it was at hand. John the Baptist came on the scene preaching to Israel and calling the nation to repentance. Matthew 3:1-2 states, *"Now in those days John the Baptist came, preaching in the wilderness of Judea, saying, 'Repent, for the kingdom of heaven is at hand.'"* It is important to note that this message was to national Israel, specifically the corrupt priesthood, calling them back into fellowship with God. If they would have repented and accepted their Messiah, Jesus, then God would have brought in the kingdom age on earth, what we often call the millennium. However, Israel, as a nation, rejected Jesus and sentenced Him to death.[1] His death and resurrection now become the basis of the gospel of the grace of God.

The promised Holy Spirit is given on the Day of Pentecost and the age of the church begins. It is during this age that the good news is preached to all men, Jew and Gentile alike. The message is not repentance from sin to bring in the kingdom, as was the case of national Israel, but to believe in the person and work of Jesus for the gift of eternal life.

The eternal gospel of Revelation 14:6-7 is the good news of God's final invitation to those alive during the tribulation period. The call is to "fear God" and to "give Him glory." Some respond in belief as is recorded in Revelation 15:3-4,

> *And they sang the song of Moses, the bond-servant of God, and the song of the Lamb, saying, "Great and marvelous are Your works, O Lord God, the Almighty; Righteous and true are Your ways, King of the nations! Who will not fear, O*

---

1 If Israel had accepted Jesus as Messiah, He still would have died and rose again as the payment for sin. How this would have been accomplished is speculation since in reality He was rejected.

Lord, and glorify Your name? For You alone are holy; For all the nations will come and worship before You, For Your righteous acts have been revealed."

In contrast, those who reject the message are seen in Revelation 16:9, *"Men were scorched with fierce heat; and they blasphemed the name of God who has the power over these plagues, and they did not repent so as to give Him glory."* Both the gospel of the kingdom and the eternal gospel emphasize seeing God in His glory. People are called to change their mind about whatever they are trusting for salvation and put their faith in God.

The book of Titus is a letter of Paul written to Titus, his child in the faith. The time is this present age, the age of the church. The grace of God that is to be proclaimed is the good news of God's grace demonstrated in the person and work of Jesus. But what is the actual content of the gospel, the message that we are to proclaim that results in eternal salvation to all who believe? I would like to explore four major areas that have to do with the gospel and then formulate a definition of the gospel we are to proclaim.

The Need. In the first three chapters of Romans, we see all the world guilty of sin. We see the Gentile condemned, the moralist condemned, and the Jew condemned. Paul's summary is found in Romans 3:23, *"For all have sinned and fall short of the glory of God."* The Greek word for sin, *hamartia*, means "to miss the mark"; thus, sin is anything that misses the mark of God's holiness and perfection. Our problem is that we are all born with a sin nature because of the fall of Adam, and we act according to our nature. Paul writes in Romans 5:12, *"Therefore, just as through one man sin entered into the world, and death through sin, and so death spread to all men, because all sinned."*

The Law. Some have mistakenly looked to the Old Testament Law as the means to correct our sin problem. However, this was never the purpose of the Law. The Law was given to Israel, God's covenant people, as a means of holiness and fellowship. The Law does bring to light Israel's failures and by extension the failures of all mankind. Paul writes in Romans 3:19, *"Now we know that whatever the Law says, it speaks to those who are under the Law, that every mouth may be closed, and all the world may become accountable to God."* The Law was never meant to be the means of justification or eternal salvation. In Galatians 2:21, Paul writes, *"I do not nullify the grace of God; for if righteousness comes through the Law, then Christ died needlessly."* In Galatians 3:24, concerning the present work of the Law, Paul writes, *"Therefore the Law has become our tutor to lead us to Christ, that we may be justified by faith."* The Law does not save us, but it does point out our inability to save ourselves and leads us to the Lord Jesus Christ.

Repentance. The Greek verb *metanoeo* means "to change one's mind" and the noun, *metanoia* simply means "a change of mind."[2] When someone believes in Jesus for eternal life, they must change their mind about whatever it was they were trusting and trust in Christ alone. Often, repentance does have the idea of turning from a particular sin or lifestyle. However, if we redefine repentance to only mean "turning from sin" and then tell unbelievers they must repent, or turn from sin, so that they can be saved, we have distorted the gospel. This clearly throws salvation back on something I do instead of simply believing in Christ for what He did. The amazing thing is that, the Gospel of John, clearly written as an evangelistic book (John 20:31), never mentions repentance, not even once! As important as repentance is in the life of an unbeliever or believer, it must not be redefined as a part of faith.[3]

The Response. The proper response to the gospel is faith! The Greek word for faith, *pisteuo*, simply means "to think to be true, or to be persuaded." Faith is taking God at His word. This word is most often translated as "believe" in the New Testament. Although some try to

---

2 Strong, J. 1996. *The exhaustive concordance of the Bible: Showing every word of the test of the common English version of the canonical books, and every occurrence of each word in regular order.* (electronic ed.). Woodside Bible Fellowship.: Ontario

3 For a detailed discussion of repentance, see Jody Dillow, chapter three in *Final Destiny, The Future Reign of the Servant Kings*, (Grace Theology Press, 2013). Also, David Anderson's chapter on repentance in *Free Grace Soteriology*, (Grace Theology Press, 2012).

redefine faith to include obedience or commitment, the Bible is clear that faith and works are exclusive. Ephesians 2:8-9 says, *"For by grace you have been saved through faith; and that not of yourselves, it is the gift of God; not of works, that no one should boast."* Salvation is the gift of God because of the finished work of Jesus. We can add nothing to that finished work. We must be clear however, that faith, in and of itself, does not save. Faith must have an object. I may have all the faith in the world in my goodness, my church membership, water baptism, or anything else *other than Jesus Christ* and that faith will not save me. Acts 4:12 is clear, *"And there is salvation in no one else; for there is no other name under heaven that has been given among men, by which we must be saved."* Jesus Himself said in John 14:6, *"I am the way, and the truth, and the life; no one comes to the Father but through Me."*

What is it that we must actually believe in order to be eternally saved, which the Bible calls being justified? One of the best known and clearest gospel verses is John 3:16, *"For God so loved the world, that He gave His only begotten Son, that whoever believes in Him shall not perish, but have eternal life."* Let's break this verse down:

1. God's love is the motivation for sending His Son Jesus. The Greek word for world is *kosmos* and refers to all mankind.
2. God's love is demonstrated in the giving of His Son, Jesus, to die for the sin of the world.
3. The required response is simple belief.
4. The promise is that, the one who believes will not perish but receives eternal life. Eternal life is received at the moment of belief.

Here then is the heart of the gospel:
- We cannot save ourselves.
- God, because of His love, graciously provided the payment for our sin in the person of His Son, Jesus Christ.
- God offers us eternal life as a free gift.
- Our response is to believe His promise and receive the gift of eternal life.

You might ask, "How do I know that Jesus paid for my sin? Does the Bible teach that the debt of my sin is truly paid in full?" It is time for us to explore what Jesus meant when he exclaimed, *"It is finished!"* in John 19:30. As we understand the finished work of Christ, we will understand how God can offer eternal salvation as a free gift!

Bringing salvation...

CHAPTER 3:

REDEMPTION, PROPITIATION, AND RECONCILIATION

John 19:30 states, *"Therefore when Jesus had received the sour wine, He said, 'It is finished!' and He bowed His head and gave up His spirit."* Three major biblical themes are related to the finished work of Christ: redemption, reconciliation, and propitiation. Lewis Sperry Chafer, founder of Dallas Theological Seminary, in his discussion of redemption, reconciliation and propitiation, states, "When the truth in each of these three doctrines as related to the unsaved is examined and segregated, and these three segregated portions are combined into one interrelated body of truth, the result is a declaration of all that enters into that which is termed the *finished work of Christ*."[1] Let's take a look at each of these three doctrines that make up the finished work of Christ.

---

1 Lewis Sperry Chafer, *Systematic Theology, Vol. III* (Dallas Seminary Press, 1948), 87.

Charles Ryrie offers this simple definition of redemption: "Redemption means liberation because of a payment made."[2] Chafer expands, "Redemption is an act of God by which He Himself pays as a ransom the price of human sin which the outraged holiness and government of God requires. Redemption undertakes the solution of the problem of sin."[3] There are actually three distinct words that are used to describe redemption in the New Testament. The first is the word *agorazo* which is defined as, "to acquire things or services in exchange for money, *buy, purchase.*"[4] A related meaning that is listed in the Greek lexicon is "to secure the rights to someone by paying a price"[5] Anderson notes, "…the price which was paid…can be none other than the death of Christ. The purchaser was God the Father. As such, those purchased now belong to Him."[6]

The second word is a variation of *agorazo.* The prefix *ex* is added, and the word is *exagorazo.* The Greek lexicon defines *exagorazo* as, "to secure deliverance of, *deliver, liberate.*[7] Now the emphasis expands from the purchase price being paid (*agorazo*) to the one purchased being delivered. All humanity is trapped, sold into slavery to sin. When Jesus shed his blood on the cross, he paid the price (*agorazo*) for the purchase of mankind in the slave market of sin. When a person believes in Christ, he or she is *exagorazo*, purchased out of the slave market of sin.

A third Greek word group is based on the word *lutron* which is defined as, "the price of release, ransom."[8] The verb form means "to free by paying a ransom, *redeem,* to liberate from an oppressive

---

2 Charles C. Ryrie, *Basic Theology*, (Victor Books, Scripture Press, 1986), 290.

3 Chafer, Vol. III, 88.

4 William Arndt et al., *A Greek-English Lexicon of the New Testament and Other Early Christian Literature* (Chicago: University of Chicago Press, 2000), 14.

5 Ibid., 14.

6 David R. Anderson, *Free Grace Soteriology* (Grace Theology Press, 2018), 80.

7 William Arndt et al., *A Greek-English Lexicon,* 343.

8 Ibid., 605.

situation, *set free.*"[9] Not only is the believer purchased out of the slave market of sin, he or she is set free! Ryrie pulls the ideas expressed in these three words together:

> Redemption may be summarized around three basic ideas.
> (1) People are redeemed *from* something; namely, from the
> marketplace or slavery of sin. (2) People are redeemed *by*
> something; namely, by the payment of a price, the blood of
> Christ. (3) People are redeemed *to* something; namely, to a
> state of freedom; and then they are called to renounce that
> freedom for slavery to the Lord who redeemed them.[10]

It is important to note that God does not *demand* that the redeemed believer serve Him. In Romans 6, Paul addresses the subject of slavery to sin versus slavery to righteousness. In verse 13 he writes, "*...do not go on presenting the members of your body to sin as instruments of unrighteousness; but present yourselves to God as those alive from the dead, and your members as instruments of righteousness to God.*" He relates the same idea in verse 19 where he says, "*For just as you presented your members as slaves to impurity and to lawlessness, resulting in further lawlessness, so now present your members as slaves to righteousness, resulting in sanctification.*" The point is that, the believer must make the decision to become a willing slave to God. He wants our obedience to come from a heart of gratitude and willing service, because we are free to do so. The Old Testament bond-servant ceremony is a beautiful picture of this willing relationship of service. Chafer sums it up well,

> Christ has not merely transferred the sinner's bondage from
> one master to another; He has purchased with the object
> in view that the ransomed one may be free. Christ will
> not hold unwilling slaves in bondage. All this is typically

---

9 William Arndt et al., *A Greek-English Lexicon,* 606.
10 Ryrie, *Basic Theology,* 292.

anticipated in Exodus 21:1-6 (cf. Deut. 15:16-17). A slave set free by his master was wholly free; but he could voluntarily remain as the slave of the master whom he loved. The new voluntary relationship was sealed by the master piercing the ear of the slave with an awl. Thus, according to type, the Christian is set free, but is privileged to yield himself wholly to the One who redeemed him."[11]

The Bible also presents two distinct dimensions of redemption. Former missionary and author C. Gordon Olson writes, "These words fall into two categories, one with an emphasis upon the objective, historical payment of the ransom price which the Lord Jesus paid through His passion, and the other, upon the subjective liberation of the individual captive from sin."[12] The objective, historical payment can be seen in 1 Peter 2:1 where Peter writes that false prophets deny *"...the Master who bought (agorazo) them."* The subjective, experiential aspect can be seen in Galatians 3:13 where Paul writes, *"Christ redeemed (exagorazō) us from the curse of the Law, having become a curse for us..."*

Olson summarizes well:

> Thus it is clear, not only that the linguistic evidence supports a distinction between the objective ransom phase of Christ's death and the subjective liberation phase in the life of the Christian, but also that such a distinction is of great value theologically. It helps to explain how the ransom price could be connected with unregenerate false teachers (2 Pet.2:1) and all mankind (1 Tim. 2:2-6), when the liberation has been effective for only a limited number. Thus, it helps resolve the tension between these two truths. Christ's ransom price was sufficient for

---

11 Chafer, Vol III. 90.

12 C. Gordon Olson, *Getting the Gospel Right* (Global Gospel Publishers, Cedar Knolls, New Jersey, 2005), 63.

all mankind and provisionally available to all, but the liberation has been effectual only for those who believe."[13]

This is helpful because we may with confidence share the gospel with unbelievers, letting them know that Jesus loves them and that His shed blood has redeemed them. However, they must respond by putting their faith in Him to receive the benefits of His redemption.

Philip B. Bliss wrote of redemption in his hymn, "I Will Sing of My Redeemer".[14] He was born on July 9, 1838. He died on December 29, 1876 in Ashtabula, Ohio in a tragic train wreck caused by a bridge collapse. He survived the initial impact but went back into the flames in an unsuccessful attempt to rescue his wife. The lyrics to one of his most loved hymns were found in his belongings after the accident:

I will sing of my Redeemer, And His wondrous love to me; On the cruel cross He suffered, From the curse to set me free

Sing, oh sing, of my Redeemer, With His blood, He purchased me. On the cross, He sealed my pardon, Paid the debt, and made me free.

I will tell the wondrous story, How my lost estate to save, In His boundless love and mercy, He the ransom freely gave.

The second doctrine that composes the finished work of Christ is reconciliation. While redemption is the work of the cross that is directed toward sin, reconciliation is directed toward man. Reconciliation comes from the Greek word *katallasso* which means "to exchange one thing for another." The Greek Lexicon defines *katallasso* as, "the exchange of hostility for a friendly relationship... God reconciles us to Himself

---

13 Olson, *Getting the Gospel Right*, 65-66.
14 https://hymnary.org/text/i_will_sing_of_my_redeemer

through Christ."[15] Ryrie states, "Reconciliation means a change of relationship from hostility to harmony and peace between two parties."[16] Mankind is the object of reconciliation since God is immutable and cannot change. God took the initiative and reconciled the world to Himself through the death of Christ.

Just as there are two distinct aspects of redemption, there are also two distinct aspects of reconciliation. Objectively and historically, the world is said to be reconciled to God by the death of Christ. Paul writes in 2 Corinthians 5:19, *"...God was in Christ reconciling the world to Himself..."* However, as believers, the moment we believe in Christ we are said to be reconciled to God. When we believe, we receive the value of Christ's reconciling death. In Romans 5:10-11, Paul writes, *"For if while we were enemies, we were reconciled to God through the death of His Son, much more, having been reconciled, we shall be saved by his life. And not only this, but we also exult in God through our Lord Jesus Christ, through whom we have now received the reconciliation."* Paul puts both aspects of reconciliation together beautifully in 2 Corinthians 5:18-20 where he writes,

> Now all these things are from God, who reconciled us to Himself through Christ and gave us the ministry of reconciliation, namely, that God was in Christ reconciling the world to Himself, not counting their trespasses against them, and He has committed to us the word of reconciliation. Therefore, we are ambassadors for Christ, as though God were making an appeal through us; we beg you on behalf of Christ, be reconciled to God.

Chafer writes, "There can be no question raised about the fact that there are two aspects of reconciliation: one wrought for all by God in His

---

15 William Arndt et al., *A Greek-English Lexicon,* 521.
16 Ryrie, Charles C., *Basic Theology,* Victor Books, Wheaton, IL, 1986, 292.

love for the world and the other wrought in the individual who believes when he believes."[17]

The third major doctrine that completes the finished work of Christ is propitiation. There are three Greek words that are variations of the root word *hileos* which is defined as, "being favorably disposed, with implication of overcoming obstacles that are unfavorable to a relationship, gracious, merciful."[18] The first word is *hilaskomai* and is only used two times in the New Testament in Luke 18:13 and Hebrews 2:17. The word is translated "merciful" in Luke 18:13 and "to make propitiation" in Hebrews 2:17. The Greek Lexicon defines *hilaskomai* as, "to cause to be favorably inclined or disposed... to eliminate impediments that alienate the deity, expiate, wipe out."[19] *Hilaskomai* emphasizes the removal of sin by the sacrifice that satisfies God. It is best translated by the English word expiation, which means to atone for something done that was wrong.

However, propitiation carries the idea of satisfying God's wrath by the death of His Son. The final two Greek words that are translated as propitiation are *hilamos* and *hilasterion*, and each is used only two times in the New Testament. *Hilamos* is used in 1 John 2:2 and 4:10 and emphasizes the sacrifice of Christ as the sin-offering that satisfied the wrath of God. In 1 John 2:2, John writes, "*...and He Himself is the propitiation for our sins; and not for ours only, but also for those of the whole world.*" In 4:10, he writes, "*In this is love, not that we loved God, but that He loved us and sent His Son to be the propitiation for our sins.*" In both of these verses, we see Jesus as the sacrificial Lamb of God who by his shed blood satisfied the wrath of God toward sin.

The word *hilasterion* also has the idea of satisfaction, but the emphasis is on the *place* of satisfaction. *Hilasterion* is also only used two times in the New Testament: Romans 3:25 and Hebrews 9:5. In Romans

---

17 Chafer, Vol III, 93.

18 William Arndt et al., *A Greek-English Lexicon*, 474.

19 Ibid., 473

3:25, speaking of Jesus, Paul writes, *"Whom God displayed publicly as a propitiation in His blood through faith..."* In Hebrews 9:5, speaking of the ark of the covenant, the author writes, *"...and above it were the cherubim of glory overshadowing the mercy seat; but of these things we cannot now speak in detail."* Here, the word *hilasterion* is translated as "mercy seat" which was the place of propitiation in the Old Testament. Note carefully the difference in these two contexts. In Hebrews, the mercy seat, the place of propitiation, was private and only accessible once a year by one person, the high priest. The inner tabernacle, known as the holy of holies, is where the ark of the covenant was located. It was hidden behind a great veil or curtain. Hebrews 9:7 states, *"...into the second, only the high priest enters, once a year, not without taking blood, which he offers for himself and for the sins of the people committed in ignorance."* Not only was the propitiation—the blood of animals sprinkled on the mercy seat—private, it also had to be repeated year after year. In the Old Testament, this covering of blood on the mercy seat is called an atonement. The word is *kapper* and means to cover or make amends. The picture painted in Hebrews 7-10 is a contrast between the old covenant of Law and the temple sacrifices that had to be repeated over and over and the final, complete, finished sacrifice of Christ. Hebrews 10:10-12 summarizes the argument,

> *By this will we have been sanctified through the offering of the body of Jesus Christ once for all. Every priest stands daily ministering and offering time after time the same sacrifices, which can never take away sins; but He, having offered one sacrifice for sins for all time, SAT DOWN AT THE RIGHT HAND OF GOD.*

When Jesus sat down at the right hand of God, He was indicating that His work was finished. He had made the final complete, satisfactory payment for sin! It is interesting that the word atonement is never used in the New Testament. I believe it is because the sacrifice of Christ was not an atonement, in the Old Testament sense of a covering of sin, but the complete final payment for the sins of all time. Gordon Olsen writes,

> To continue to call the passion of Christ 'the atonement,' when in fact the word is never used in the New Testament, is not conductive to the precision for which the science of theology should be known... The term atonement is especially objectionable since it only describes the Levitical sacrifices, which were not a final dealing with sin and only anticipated the saving death of Christ.[20]

This is the point of Hebrews 9:26, *"...but now once at the consummation of the ages He has been manifested to put away sin by the sacrifice of Himself."*

In light of the use of *hilasterion* in Hebrews 9:5, we can now see the contrast in Romans 3:25, the second usage of this word. Paul writes, *"Whom God displayed publicly as a propitiation in His blood through faith..."* While the mercy seat, the place of propitiation in the Old Testament, was accessible only by the high priest, in contrast the cross, the place of propitiation in the New Testament is public and accessible to all! In Mark 15:37-38 we read, *"And Jesus uttered a loud cry, and breathed His last. And the veil of the temple was torn in two from top to bottom."* Now access to God through the finished work of His Son Jesus is open to everyone. In the two words *hilasmos* and *hilasterion*, we see Jesus as both the perfect sacrifice that satisfied the wrath of God and also the very place of the sacrifice where man may come to meet God.

As with redemption and reconciliation, there is a twofold dimension of propitiation:

1. The world

Christ is said to be the propitiation for the sins of the world. There is no qualification here. The world has been covered by Christ's

---

20 Olson, *Getting the Gospel Right,* 70.

propitiation regardless of how many believe it. Chafer makes this point clear:

> Thus it is revealed that God is propitious, not when faith of confession has made Him so, but because of the death of His Son. Neither sinners nor sinning saints are appointed to the task of propitiating God. Christ has accomplished that perfectly, and the door into the grace of God is open wide."[21]

Olson states, "How wonderful to know that God is perfectly satisfied with the sacrifice of Christ for the sins of the whole world."[22]

2. Believers

Jesus, in His own Person, "...has also become an infinitely sufficient 'meeting place' between a Holy God and a sinful man, but only for believers."[23] We see this clearly in Romans 3:25 when Paul says that Christ was set forth as a mercy seat *"through faith"*. Zane Hodges states,

> So *hilasterion* in Rom. 3:25 does not so much describe a position as it does a function... whenever an unsaved sinner comes to God through God's chosen Mediator, Jesus fulfills the function of the Old Covenant mercy seat by becoming the genuine meeting place between God and the believing sinner. In other words, man and God really meet in Jesus Christ when saving faith occurs. Unlike the inanimate mercy seat of Moses' day, the risen and living Jesus Christ 'introduces' the sinner to God. And He does so by bestowing eternal life – God's life – on the one who believes, so that the believer knows God (see John 17:3). God on His part bestows His perfect righteousness on the believer."[24]

---

21 Chafer, Vol III, 96.
22 Olson, 62-63.
23 Hodges, Zane, *Grace in Focus*, (Grace Evangelical Society, July/August 2006), 3.
24 Hodges, *Grace in Focus*, 4.

So we see that propitiation is the work of God by which His wrath is satisfied by the death of His Son, the Lord Jesus Christ, on the cross. This propitiation is universal in that the sins of the world are propitiated (1 Jn 2:2) by Jesus Christ's sacrifice but specific, in that through faith, the believer enters into a relationship with God through Jesus, the living Mercy Seat (Rom 3:25).

The implications of these three great doctrines, which compose the finished work of Christ, are amazing. God, because of His love for mankind, provided complete salvation through His Son. Christ's death on the cross purchased us out of the slave market of sin, reconciled us to God and satisfied God's righteous wrath toward sin. Each of these doctrines has a specific purpose or we might say is directed at a specific goal. Redemption is directed toward our sin. The sin issue is settled because we are bought with a price and redeemed out of the slavery of sin. Reconciliation is directed toward man. The blood of Christ broke down the barrier and enmity that separates man from God. Propitiation is directed toward God. Christ's blood completely satisfies the wrath of God and opens access to God through faith.

The power of the gospel rests on the finished work of Christ. We may now, with confidence, tell the lost person that God loves them, He has made provision for their sins, and He now offers them eternal life by simple faith in His Son, Jesus. The work is done! The price has been paid! The offer of life is there for all who will believe.

Bringing salvation...

CHAPTER 4:
JUSTIFICATION, IMPUTATION, REGENERATION

We have seen the wonderful benefits of the finished work of Christ both to the world and to all who put their faith in Him. When a person believes in Christ, there are a number of things that immediately occur. Lewis Sperry Chafer writes that there are "...thirty-three stupendous works of God which together comprise the salvation of a soul..."[1] We have already looked at three of those works: redemption, reconciliation, and propitiation. In this chapter, we will look at three more "works" or doctrines that relate specifically to the believer.

The first is the concept of justification. Understanding justification is critical to understanding the grace of God and the gospel. Key issues are raised by Anderson when he questions, "Is justification something

---

1 Chafer, Vol. III, 234.

that occurs instantaneously, or is it a process occurring over a period of time? Is this a divine act by which God 'declares' a person righteous or a process by which He 'makes' them righteous?"[2] The answers to these questions are the basis for the differences between Catholic and Protestant theology. The proper understanding of justification was the critical issue that triggered Martin Luther's ninety-five theses. In his commentary on Galatians, Luther writes, "For if the article of justification be once lost, then is all true Christian doctrine lost."[3] Anderson lists four primary distinctions that must be settled if justification is to be understood:

1. "Made righteous" (infused) versus "declared" righteous (imputed);
2. Instantaneous versus a process;
3. Faith alone or faith plus meritorious works; and
4. Forensic versus existential.[4]

To understand the above distinctions, we must start with a brief word study. The Greek verb for "justify" is *dikaioo*. The Greek Lexicon gives the following range of meanings:[5]

1. "to take up a legal cause, show justice, do justice, take up a cause."
2. "to render a favorable verdict, *vindicate*."
3. "to cause someone to be released from personal or institutional claims that are no longer to be considered pertinent or valid, *make free/pure*."
4. "to demonstrate to be morally right, *prove to be right*."

Paul uses this word fifteen times in the book of Romans. Beginning in chapter 3 verse 20 through chapter 5, the great passage on justification

---

2 Anderson, *Free Grace Theology*, 99.
3 Martin Luther, <u>*Commentary on Galatians*</u> (Oak Harbor, WA: Logos Research Systems, Inc., 1997), 26–40.
4 Anderson, *Free Grace Soteriology*, 110.
5 William Arndt, Frederick W. Danker, et al., *A Greek English Lexicon*, 249.

by faith alone, Paul uses the word nine times. In Romans 3:20, he writes, *"…by the works of the Law no flesh will be justified in His sight; for through the Law comes the knowledge of sin."* This Scripture clearly rules out works as a part of justification before God. Verse 24, speaking of the sinner who has fallen short of God's glory, declares that he or she is *"…justified as a gift by His grace through the redemption which is in Christ Jesus."* This verse emphasizes the third lexicon definition of *dikaioo* and is further validated by the use of the word for "redemption," which means "to loose or set free." In verse 26, based on the redemption of verse 24 and the propitiation of verse 25, God is said to be, *"…just and the justifier of the one who has faith in Jesus."* This speaks of definition two, "to render a favorable verdict, to vindicate." Paul summarizes in verse 28, *"For we maintain that a man is justified by faith apart from works of the Law."* In Romans 4:5, a legal accounting term is used to describe the result of justification: righteousness *credited* to the account of the believer. Olson summarizes, "The Greek word clearly has a forensic, legal connotation and was in the language of the courts. Paul presented the truth of God's declaration of the sinner as righteous in His sight based on faith alone, without works of any kind."[6] The word *forensic* is a legal term that means "relating to courts of law." Anderson notes, "From both the OT and NT contexts which support a courtroom setting for the use of 'to justify,' it would seem to go without saying that the meaning of this word is forensic."[7]

Back to our four primary distinctions, we can say with biblical authority that justification means: 1) to be declared righteous, 2) it is an instantaneous process, 3) it is by faith alone, and 4) it is forensic in nature. L. M. Peterson, in his article on "Justification," summarizes well,

> In the Scriptures…the terms "justification" or "to justify" are used in a special Biblical, forensic, or judicial sense, "to declare or pronounce righteous," not to make righteous…

---

6 Olsen, *Beyond Calvinism & Arminianism*, 124.
7 Anderson, *Free Grace Soteriology*, 114.

It is a declarative act of the God of grace by which He declares sinners free from the guilt and consequences of their sin through faith in the atonement of Christ... A just man is not pronounced just because he is just, but a sinful man is pronounced just because his sins have been atoned for by the righteousness of Christ.[8]

In God's courtroom, when a person believes in Jesus Christ, God—because of Christ's finished work—justifies the believer and declares him or her righteous. God does not make the believer righteous but credits His righteousness to the believer's account.

But what about the actual state of a believer? After all, John writes in 1 John 1:8, *"If we say that we have no sin, we are deceiving ourselves, and the truth is not in us."* How can we be both righteous and sinners at the same time? The Latin phrase, often attributed to Martin Luther, *simul iustus et peccator* translates as, "simultaneous righteous and sinner." Regarding this phrase, Anderson writes, "The believer is righteous in principle, but sinful in practice. This is what we call righteous in our *position* in Christ, but sinful in our *condition* on earth."[9] Anderson explains,

The distinction necessary to understand this seeming paradox of being just and sinful at the same time is between *position* and *condition*. It is in our position (our standing) in Christ that we are truly righteous. Our account in heaven has already been credited (λογίζομαι, "imputed," is an accounting term) to our account in heaven. This is not fictional, and it is not an infusion of character into the believer. It is the very righteousness of Christ *in us* credited to our account in heaven by virtue of our position in Him. Our character revealed on earth is our condition.

---

8 Lorman Peterson, "Justification," *The Zondervan Pictorial Encyclopedia of the Bible, Volume Three* (Grand Rapids, Michigan, Zondervan Publishing House), 764-65.
9 Anderson, *Free Grace Soteriology*, 106.

This distinction between position and condition is not a peripheral truth in the Christian life. It is central and crucial because it is only as we focus on our position in Him that our condition begins to conform to His character (see 2 Cor 3:18). We *become* what we *think about* and appropriate for ourselves.[10]

Our *position* in Christ is confirmed by numerous Scriptures. In Romans 3:21-22, Paul speaks about "a righteousness of God" which is appropriated by faith. Most English Bibles translate the phrase, "the righteousness of God," but in the Greek text there is no definite article. Paul is not emphasizing that God is righteous, although of course He is, but instead that God's very righteousness is imputed to the believer. In verses 25 and 26, God's righteousness is demonstrated because he can now justify the one who has faith in Jesus. God is just to do so because the believer now has the very righteousness of God imputed to his account.

In Romans 5:1, Paul writes, *"Therefore, having been justified by faith, we have peace with God through our Lord Jesus Christ."* Clearly, *having been justified* is an event that has already happened. In Greek grammar, this is an *aorist participle.* Wallace writes, *"Aorist participles* usually suggest *antecedent* time to that of the main verb (i.e., *past* time in a *relative* sense)."[11] In other words, our peace with God is because we have been justified.

Another passage that emphasizes our position in Christ is Ephesians 1:20 and the parallel verse in 2:6. Paul writes in 1:20, speaking of God's might brought about in Christ, *"...when He raised Him from the dead and seated Him at His right hand in the heavenly places."* This is Christ's present position, seated at the right hand of the Father. Now notice in 2:6 that God *"...raised us up with Him, and seated us with Him in the heavenly places in Christ Jesus."* Because we are in Christ, our *position* is

---

10 Anderson, *Free Grace Soteriology*, 116.
11 Daniel B. Wallace, *Greek Grammar; Beyond the Basics: An Exegetical Syntax of the New Testament* (Grand Rapids, Michigan, Zondervan, 1996), 555.

seated with Him in the heavens. Our *condition* is still here on earth and is affected by how we live our lives in light of our *position*. We should understand Romans 5:9 in the same light of *position* and *condition*. Paul writes, *"Much more then, having now been justified by His blood, we shall be saved from the wrath of God through Him."* Having been justified is our *position*! It is in the past, a completed action. However, *we shall be saved* speaks to future events, or our sanctification—our *condition*. The power to live the Christian life comes from understanding who we are in Christ and that our eternal destiny is forever settled—our *position*. That security gives us the freedom to serve Christ out of a grace/love relationship instead of a law/fear relationship. As we reflect on our *position* in Christ, we will be motivated to bring our *condition* into conformity with His word.

This brings us to the doctrine of imputation, which further helps to explain justification. The Greek word for imputation is *logizomai* and is translated "to reckon, to calculate, to credit, or to take into account." The Greek Lexicon defines *logizomai* as, "to determine by mathematical process, *reckon, calculate;*"[12] specifically to, *"put on someone's account, charge to someone."*[13] In Romans 4:3, Paul writes, *"For what does the Scripture say? Abraham believed God, and it was credited to him as righteousness."* As a matter of fact, Paul uses this word eleven times in Romans 4 to make it crystal clear that righteousness is *credited* to our account. Paul quotes both Genesis 15:6 and Psalm 32:1-2 because the Septuagint uses *logizomai* to translate the Hebrew word for 'reckon' in each of these verses. Psalm 32 is one of David's penitential psalms that he wrote after he sinned greatly (Psalm 51). Paul not only shows that David believed in imputed righteousness but also that David's sin did not cancel his justification. In Romans 4:9-12, Paul establishes that Abraham was justified, prior to being circumcised and proves that all people, Gentile and Jew, have always been justified by faith. Paul writes,

---

12 William Arndt, Frederick W. Danker, et al., *A Greek-English Lexicon*, 597.
13 Ibid.

"Is this blessing then upon the circumcised, or upon the uncircumcised also? For we say, Faith was reckoned to Abraham as righteousness. How then was it reckoned? While he was circumcised, or uncircumcised? Not while circumcised, but while uncircumcised." This imputation of righteousness to the sinner's account is one of the major imputations taught in Scripture. Olsen writes,

> This truth of imputation becomes even clearer when seen in the light of the appropriate synonyms, as 'reckon, count, account, or charge.' Paul referred to a two-fold imputation: of the believer's sin to Christ the sinbearer, and of Christ's righteousness to believing sinners (Rom 4:1-8; Col 2:13-14). Thus, not only are all believers' sins charged to Christ's account when He bore them on the cross, but also His righteousness is accounted to believers to give perfect standing with God. The whole argument of Romans is based upon this truth.[14]

The imputations are as follows:

1. The sin of the race to Christ. Central passages are 2 Corinthians 5:21, 1 Peter 2:24 and Isaiah 53:5-6, 11. Although the word 'impute' is not used, similar terms like 'made him to be sin', 'laid on Him', and 'bore our sins' clearly imply imputation. This is JUDICIAL IMPUTATION since Christ was sinless yet took our sins upon Himself.

2. The righteousness of God to the believer. The book of Romans is central, especially chapter 4, as well as 2 Corinthians 5:21 and Philippians 3:9. Chafer writes,

> This imputation constitutes the Christian's acceptance and standing before God. It is the only righteousness that God

---

14 Olsen, *Beyond Calvinism*, 126.

ever accepts for salvation and by it alone may one enter heaven.... The apostolic phrase the *righteousness of God* (Rom. 1:17; 3:22; 10:3), then, means a righteousness from rather than the mere fact that God Himself is righteous. In Romans 3:10 it is declared that none among men are in the sight of God righteous; hence an imputed righteousness is the only hope for men on this earth. Regarding the hope of imputed righteousness, the Apostle wrote: "...not having mine own righteousness, which is of the law, but that which is through the faith of Christ, the righteousness which is of God by faith" (Phil 3:9).[15]

Just as Christ's finished work on the cross is the basis for the remission of sin, it is also the legal basis for God to impute His righteousness to everyone who believes in Christ. It is important to understand that we are not *made righteous* but are *declared righteous!* That is, righteousness is reckoned or posted to our account on the basis of faith, not on something we do. *"But to the one who does not work, but believes in Him who justifies the ungodly, his faith is reckoned as righteousness (Rom 4:5)."*

3. Some theologians see a third major imputation in Romans 5:12, which is Adam's sin imputed to mankind. There are actually three major views as to the meaning of the phrase, *"death spread to all men, because all sinned."* View one is *Personal Sin* and states that every individual commits personal sin. View two is *Original Sin* and states that from Adam on, everyone born inherits a corrupt nature. Anderson writes, "...when Adam sinned, a constitutional change took place in his person... From then on a corrupt nature, usually referred to as the sin nature, was resident within

---

15 Chafer, Vol. III, 192.

him. This corrupt nature was then passed down to all of his descendants, Hence, every individual born is spiritually dead, separated from God, because of the sin nature within him."[16] The third view is *Imputed Sin*, sometimes called 'Federal Headship.' This view sees Adam as acting as a representative for the whole human race. Anderson explains, "Adam, as federal head of the human race, sinned; as our representative, sin was charged to the account of the entire human race and death came to the whole human race."[17] I personally believe the *Original Sin* view best fits the context of Roman 5:12. Anderson summarizes, "Romans 5:12-13 and 19 thus exclude the forensic categories of personal imputation or federal headship as the root cause of 'all sinned' in favor of the inherited condition of sinners by constitution, that is, the 'sin nature' or 'original sin.'"[18]

We have seen that the justified believer rests securely in his or her position in Christ, declared righteous in the courtroom of God. This righteousness is imputed (*logizomai*) to our account so that God sees us as righteousness in His Son.

The third doctrine that relates to our eternal salvation is *Regeneration*. The actual Greek word for regeneration (*palingenesia*) is used only twice in the New Testament (Matt 19:28; Ti 3:5) and means "to be born again". The Lexicon defines *palingenesia* as, "experience of a complete change of life, rebirth of a redeemed person."[19] In John 3:3, John uses the words "born again," (*gennao anothen*) which literally translates "born from above" to denote the new birth. Thus, regeneration is the fact of the 'new birth' of which Jesus spoke to Nicodemus in John

---

16 Anderson, *Free Grace Soteriology*, 39.
17 Ibid., 40.
18 Ibid., 41.
19 William Arndt, Frederick W. Danker, et al., *A Greek English Lexicon*, 752.

chapter 3. It is the imparting of the divine nature and the resulting divine sonship to all believers. Chafer lists five facts of regeneration:

1. a new life has been thereby begotten which is eternal;
2. that life is the divine nature;
3. the believer is begotten by the Spirit;
4. God the Father becomes his legitimate Father;
5. therefore, all believers are heirs of God and joint heirs with Christ.

On the human side, regeneration is conditioned simply on faith (Jn 1:12-13; Gal 3:26).[20]

We have looked at three major doctrines and how they relate to a person when he or she believes in Jesus Christ. We saw that justification is a courtroom term and means that a person is legally declared righteous the moment he or she believes in Jesus Christ. This righteousness of God is imputed to the believer's account so that God sees the believer in His Son and possessing the very righteousness of Christ. The believer is born again (spiritually) and receives a new nature when he or she believes in Christ. However, the order of salvation, called the *ordo salutis*, is debated among theologians. Most consistent Reformed theologians believe that a person must be regenerated by God *before* he or she can believe. This also raises questions about who can be saved. Does the offer of eternal life extend to all people or to only some? We will explore this subject next!

---

20 Chafer, Vol. III, 264-265.

To all men...

CHAPTER 5:

GRACE OFFERED TO ALL

Wwhat does it mean that grace brings salvation to all men? Here are some interpretations that have been offered:

1. All mankind will be saved (Universalism).
2. All men are now savable.
3. Only those who believe receive the benefits of salvation.
4. All refers to the elect, not all mankind.

Admittedly, this is a difficult subject to boil down into a brief chapter. Theologians have argued for centuries over what it means for salvation to be offered to all men. I will try to briefly narrow down the interpretations into three main camps: Reformed (Calvinism), Arminian, and Free Grace. Theologically, the extent of the atonement answers the above questions. However, there are two other areas of the atonement that are important. David Allen, seminary professor and theologian, in his book *The Extent of the Atonement: A Historical and Critical Review*, writes, "…it is vital to recognize and distinguish between three major areas comprising the subject of the atonement: (1) intent, (2) extent, and (3) application. One cannot consider the extent question apart from the question of intent and application."[1] The *intent* of the atonement asks the question, "What was Christ's saving purpose in providing an atonement? Did he equally or unequally desire the salvation of every Man?"[2] Did He intend, by His death, to make salvation possible for all people or just some? The *extent* of the atonement, "… answers the question, for whose sins was Christ punished? There are only two possible answers: (1) He died for the sins of all humanity… (2) He died for the sins of the elect only (limited atonement), as he only intends their salvation."[3] The *application* of the atonement, "…answers the question, 'When is the atonement applied to the sinner?'"[4] Allen gives three possible answers:

1. It is applied in the eternal decree of God. This is the view of many hyper-Calvinists.

2. It is applied at the cross to all the elect at the time of Jesus's death.

3. It is applied at the moment the sinner exercises faith in Christ.[5]

Allen summarizes, "When it comes to the question of the extent of the atonement, one needs to have all the options on the table and all of them rightly represented before beginning to discriminate between them and see which viewpoint is true biblically."[6]

We will begin by looking at numerous passages of Scripture that seem to indicate that salvation is offered to all men. That is, the *intent* was the salvation of all men, the *extent* of His payment was for the sins

---

1 David L. Allen, *The Extent of the Atonement: A Historical and Critical Review* (Nashville, TN, B&H Academic, 2016) XIX.
2 Ibid.
3 Ibid., XX
4 Ibid.
5 Ibid.
6 Ibid., XXI

of all mankind, and the *application* of the payment is realized at the moment of faith. After looking at these texts, we will briefly look at the interpretations from a Reformed (Calvinism), Arminian, and Free Grace perspective.

1. John 1:9-12. *"There was the true Light which, coming into the world, enlightens every man. He was in the world, and the world was made through Him, and the world did not know Him. He came to His own, and those who were His own did not receive Him. But as many as received Him, to them He gave the right to become children of God, even to those who believe in His name."* Constable explains,

> The point is that Jesus as the "true Light" affects everyone. Everyone lives under the spotlight of God's illuminating revelation in Jesus Christ since the Incarnation (cf. 1 John 1). His light clarifies the sinfulness and spiritual need of human beings. Those who respond to this convicting revelation positively experience salvation. Those who reject it and turn from the light will …experience eternal damnation.[7]

2. John 1:29. *"The next day he saw Jesus coming to him and said "Behold, the Lamb of God who takes away the sin of the world!"* Some try to redefine "world," *kosmos* in the Greek, as only the world of the elect. Constable comments, "John usually used the word world (Gr. *kosmos*) in a negative sense in this Gospel (cf. v. 10; 7:7; 14:17, 22, 27, 30; 15:18–19; 16:8, 20, 33; 17:6, 9, 14). It does not refer to this planet as a planet, but to the inhabited earth fallen in sin and in rebellion against God. It is the world of humanity darkened by sin."[8] In some form, the sin of the entire world has been taken away!

3. John 3:16-17. *"For God so loved the world, that He gave His only begotten Son, that whoever believes in Him shall not perish, but have*

---

7 Tom Constable, *Tom Constable's Expository Notes on the Bible* (Galaxie Software, 2003), Jn 1:9.
8 Ibid.

eternal life. For God did not send the Son into the world to judge the world, but that the world might be saved through Him." God's provision of salvation is based on His love for the world (*kosmos*). There exists the possibility that the *world might be saved through Him.*

4. John 6:33, 40. *"For the bread of God is that which comes down out of heaven, and gives life to the world...For this is the will of My Father, that everyone who beholds the Son and believes in Him will have eternal life, and I Myself will raise him up on the last day."* Here we see that life is available to the world and is received by belief in Jesus.

5. John 12:46. *"I have come as Light into the world, so that everyone who believes in Me will not remain in darkness."* The Light is available to the world and all who believe are delivered from the darkness.

6. John 16:7-8. *"But I tell you the truth, it is to your advantage that I go away; for if I do not go away, the Helper will not come to you; but if I go, I will send Him to you. And He, when He comes, will convict the world concerning sin and righteousness and judgment."* Part of the Holy Spirit's ministry is convicting the world.

7. 1 John 2:2. *"...and He Himself is the propitiation for our sins; and not for ours only, but also for those of the whole world."* Here, believers are contrasted with those of the world system. This verse clearly states that Christ's death was unlimited, that is, He paid for the sins of the whole world.

8. 2 Peter 3:9. *"The Lord is not slow about His promise, as some count slowness, but is patient toward you, not wishing for any to perish but for all to come to repentance."* Constable's comments are helpful. He writes,

> We know that God desires that everyone have enough freedom to believe or disbelieve the gospel. He desires this more strongly than He desires that everyone be saved. Otherwise, everyone would end up believing in Christ. But that will not happen (v. 7; Matt. 25:46)... Nevertheless, God sincerely desires ...that every person

come to salvation. Similarly, God also desires that everyone be holy, but not everyone will be holy.

It is more important to God, therefore, that people be free moral agents, and freely and willingly make the choice to accept or reject His grace, than that everyone accept it without the ability to make that choice. God is so sovereign and in control that His ultimate will still is accomplished even though He gives humans the ability to make choices. Our freedom is real but limited. We can choose some things but not others (e.g., to fly like birds)[9]

9. 1 Timothy 2:3-6. *"This is good and acceptable in the sight of God our Savior,* **who desires all men to be saved and to come to the knowledge of the truth.** *For there is one God, and one mediator also between God and men, the man Christ Jesus, who gave Himself* **as a ransom for all,** *the testimony given at the proper time."* Allen explains, "Paul links God's purpose and desire for the salvation of all people with the atonement as the means whereby that can be accomplished. The text explicitly teaches God's universal saving will…the text clearly affirms a universal atonement – 'Christ died for all'."[10]

It certainly seems that by taking these texts at face value, they all affirm a universal atonement. Theologians from the Reformed, Calvinist position fall back on their theological system to interpret these texts. They rely on what is called the *ordo salutis*, a Latin phrase meaning "order of salvation." Anderson notes, "This refers to either the temporal or logical sequence in which the various elements of salvation are imparted to the believer, from his calling to his glorification."[11] Reformed theology has tended to emphasize the *ordo salutis* to

---

9 Tom Constable, *Tom Constable's Expository Notes on the Bible* (Galaxie Software, 2003), 2 Pe 3:9.

10 David L. Allen, *The Atonement* (Nashville, Tennessee, B&H Academic, 2019) 226-27.

11 David R. Anderson. *Free Grace Soteriology.* (Maitland, FL: Xulon Press, 2010), 119.

defend its understanding of God's divine work in salvation. Reformed theologian Louis Berkhof writes,

> The *ordo salutis* describes the process by which the work of salvation, wrought in Christ, is subjectively realized in the hearts and lives of sinners. It aims at describing in their logical order, and also in their interrelations, the various movements of the Holy Spirit in the application of the work of redemption. The emphasis is not on what man does in appropriation of the grace of God but on what God does in applying it.[12]

In his article entitled "SOLUS, SOLA: Constructing a Christocentric faith model of the 'ordo saiutis'", André van Oudtshoorn states, "The *ordo salutis* directly impacts on the way in which a large segment of Christians appropriate the message of salvation and communicate it to the world."[13] For Reformed theologians, the development of the *ordo salutis* was a means of defending their view of God's sovereignty and His sovereign grace. Meanwhile, in his book *Faith and Justification*, Reformed theologian G. C. Berkouwer writes, "It appears to us…that the critics of the *ordo salutis* often fail to see that the motive behind it was the maintenance of the sovereignty of God's grace. The origin of the *ordo salutis* was closely connected with a virulent defense of the Gospel."[14] Reformed theology elevates God's sovereignty above all of His other attributes, and their system has come to be defined by the acronym TULIP, which stands for Total depravity, Unconditional election, Limited atonement, Irresistible grace, and Perseverance of the saints. Concerning total depravity, Berkhof writes, "The inherent corruption

---

12 L. Berkhof, *Systematic Theology* (Grand Rapids, MI: Wm. B. Eerdmans publishing co., 1938), 415-416.

13 André van Oudtshoorn. "SOLUS, SOLA: Constructing a Christocentric faith model of the 'ordo salutis'." (*Verbum Et Ecclesia* 35, no.1, January 2014): 1-9. EBSCOhost (accessed October 4, 2017).

14 Berkouwer, *Faith and Justification*, 26.

extends to every part of man's nature...there is no spiritual good...in relation to God in the sinner at all.... With respect to its effect on man's spiritual powers, it is called total inability."[15] Echoing Berkhof, David Steele and Curtis Thomas write, "As a result of this inborn corruption, the natural man is totally unable to do anything spiritually good; thus Calvinists speak of man's 'total inability'...the sinner is so spiritually bankrupt that *he can do nothing pertaining to his salvation.*"[16] According to Calvinism, man is so spiritually dead that he cannot believe the gospel unless God first regenerates him. Therefore, a key component of the Reformed *ordo salutis* is that regeneration must precede faith in Christ. Arthur Pink writes, "The new birth is solely the work of God the Spirit and man has no part or lot in it...No corpse can reanimate itself...Faith is not the cause of the new birth, but the consequence of it...for a dead man cannot believe anything."[17] R.C. Sproul writes, "No man has the power to raise himself from spiritual death. Divine assistance is needed and needed absolutely."[18] He continues, "Is regeneration a monergistic work of God, or is it a synergistic work that requires cooperation between man and God?"[19] Sproul answers his question by stating, "It is probably true that the majority of professing Christians in the world today believe that the order of our salvation is this: Faith precedes regeneration. We are exhorted to *choose* to be born again. But telling a man to choose rebirth is like exhorting a corpse to choose resurrection. The exhortation falls upon deaf ears."[20] It is noteworthy that Sproul represents faith as something we *choose* to do rather than a simple response to the message of the gospel. In Reformed theology, if man is capable of exercising faith,

---

15 Berkhof, *Systematic Theology,* 247.

16 David N. Steele and Curtis C. Thomas, *The Five Points of Calvinism: Defined, Defended, Documented*, International Library of Philosophy and Theology: Biblical and Theological Studies (Philadelphia: Presbyterian and Reformed Pub. Co., 1963), 25.

17 Arthur Walkington Pink, *The Sovereignty of God* (Blacksburg, Va.: Wilder, 2008), 1.

18 R. C. Sproul, *The Mystery of the Holy Spirit* (Wheaton, Ill.: Tyndale House Publishers, ©1990), 102-103.

19 Ibid., 104.

20 Ibid.

then somehow, he has added to God's provision. Therefore, God must be the one who accomplishes everything, even giving the gift of faith. Steele and Thomas write, "This is the one point of Calvinistic soteriology which the 'five points' are concerned to establish…namely, that sinners do not save themselves in any sense at all, but that salvation, first and last, whole and entire, past, present and future, is of the Lord, to whom be the glory forever: amen."[21] As we have seen, total depravity, as defined by the Calvinist, means total inability and necessitates that God must regenerate a man before he can believe. The rest of TULIP logically flows from this understanding of total depravity. Election must be unconditional since God is the one who regenerates the sinner, and that can only be by His sovereign choice. Sproul writes, "Reformed theology sees faith as the result of election. This is the fundamental difference between conditional election and unconditional election."[22] Furthermore, grace must be irresistible since God regenerates apart from the will of man. B. B. Warfield summarizes, "When rightly considered, Calvinism, with its doctrines of election and irresistible grace, is the only system which can make credible the salvation of any sinner since in these doctrines alone are embodied in its purity the evangelical principles that salvation is from God alone and from him only in the immediate working of his grace."[23] The final two points of TULIP flow logically from the others. If God chooses a particular group, the elect, to save, then Christ's death on the cross was only for that particular group. It is inconceivable, to the Calvinist, that Christ would shed His blood for those He never intended to save. Warfield states clearly,

> Calvinism insists that the saving operations of God are directed in every case immediately to the individuals who are saved. Particularism in the processes of salvation

---

21 Steele and Thomas, *Calvinism*, 23.

22 R. C. Sproul, *What Is Reformed Theology? Understanding the Basics*, repackaged ed. (Grand Rapids, Michigan: Baker Books, 2016), 170.

23 B.B. Warfield, *The Plan of Salvation* (Lexington, KY: Bowker, 2017), 50.

becomes thus the mark of Calvinism...God the Lord, in his saving operations, deals not generally with mankind at large, but particularly with the individuals who are actually saved.... The denial of particularism is constructively the denial of the immediacy of saving grace, that is, of evangelicalism, and of the supernaturalism of salvation, that is, of Christianity itself. It is logically the total rejection of Christianity.[24]

The final point, perseverance of the saints, is necessary in the system. If God is the One who elects, regenerates, and calls, then He will certainly protect and take His elect ones on to glorification. Logically, perseverance of the saints, as defined in Calvinism, means that every true believer will grow in his sanctification and exhibit the fruits of perseverance. The problem arises when a professed Christian does not continue to grow in the faith or back-slides in his Christian life. For the Calvinist, it is impossible that one who is elect, called, justified, and sanctified will not continue to grow and exhibit fruit throughout his life. Romans 8:28-30 is the passage most used by Reformed theologians to form their *ordo salutis*. Paul presents the following order: foreknew – predestined – called – justified – glorified. Of course, faith, repentance, regeneration, and sanctification are not mentioned in this passage, which leads to speculation about how and where they fit in the *ordo*. Anderson presents the following as representative of the Reformed *ordo salutis*:

1. Election. God chose some to receive eternal life from eternity past irrespective of His prior knowledge that they would choose to receive Christ.
2. Calling. This calling is irresistible.
3. Regeneration. This is accomplished by the Holy Spirit apart from any activity of man.

---

24 Warfield, *The Plan of Salvation*, 63.

4. Repentance. Through the power of the Holy Spirit within them, the regenerate turns away from all sin.

5. Faith. The regenerate now makes a personal decision to receive Christ as Savior and Lord of their lives.

6. Justification. The new believer is now declared righteous in the courtroom of heaven.

7. Sanctification. The justified person now begins the process of being made holy by the Holy Spirit. Though there are ups and downs, the 'trend line' is always up.

8. Preservation. Because it is God's power which preserves the elect, they cannot fall away from the faith. Therefore, the saints persevere until the end of their lives.

9. Glorification. When Christ returns, the elect are permanently rid of all aspects of the Fall; that is, they are glorified.[25]

Anderson reflects,

> What difference does this order make? Primarily, it is an issue of divine sovereignty and human responsibility. Those heavy on sovereignty want to take man right out of the picture. So God does everything to shape the pitiful lump of clay into the image of His Son to the point that the clay has no mind, emotion, or will in the matter whatsoever. To say he does, would be to undermine the doctrine of divine sovereignty.[26]

However, many outside the Reformed camp have trouble with the idea that God eternally condemns men for not believing, but at the same time has chosen not to give them the ability to believe. The theological system called Arminianism is named after the Dutch theologian, Jacobus Arminius. Author of *The Other Side of Calvinism* Laurence Vance

---

25 Anderson, *Free Grace Soteriology*, 122-123.
26 Ibid.

writes, "Arminius was just as orthodox on the cardinal doctrines of the Christian Faith as any Calvinist, ancient or modern."[27] Vance continues, "It is to be remembered that the academy in Geneva where Arminius received his theological training was the very school founded by Calvin. Arminius studied under Beza, the successor of Calvin."[28] While studying at Geneva under Beza, Arminius found himself in the middle of the predestination issue and was asked to refute a book written against Calvinism. Vance notes that during his preparations to refute the anti-Calvinist book, "Arminius underwent a theological transformation and became a convert to the very opinions which he had been requested to combat and refute."[29] Vance summarizes,

> It is Arminius' interpretation of predestination that is the crux of his argument with Calvin. Rather than applying predestination to unbelievers (as did Calvin), Arminius applied it only to believers.... Arminius summarized his views of predestination as "an eternal and gracious decree of God in Christ, by which He determines to justify and adopt believers, and to endow them with life eternal, but to condemn unbelievers and impenitent persons.... Arminius reduces the controversy over Calvinism to two...questions: "Do we believe, because we have been elected?" or "Are we elected, because we believe?" This was the main issue in Arminius' day; it was the main issue in the subsequent Calvinism-Arminianism debates; it remains the main issue in these same debates today.[30]

---

27 Laurence M. Vance, *The Other Side of Calvinism*, rev. ed. (Pensacola, FL: Vance Publications, ©1999), 126.
28 Ibid., 132.
29 Ibid., 134.
30 Ibid., 138.

Because of the importance of personal faith in salvation, faith becomes an essential element in the Arminian *ordo salutis*. Ben Henshaw writes,

> The main difference between the Arminian and Calvinist *ordo* concerns faith and regeneration. Strictly speaking, faith is not part of salvation in the Arminian *ordo* since it is the condition that is met prior to God's act of saving. All that follows faith is salvation in the Arminian *ordo* while in the Calvinist *ordo* faith is the result of salvation in some sense. What follows is how I see the Arminian *ordo salutis*:
>
> > Prevenient grace
> > Faith
> > [Union with Christ]
> > Justification
> > Regeneration
> > Sanctification
> > Glorification[31]

Defining the Arminian concept of "prevenient grace" in his article, "The FACTS of Salvation: A Summary of Arminian Theology/the Biblical Doctrines of Grace," Brian Abasciano writes,

> The term "prevenient" simply means "preceding." Thus, "prevenient grace" refers to God's grace that precedes salvation.... Prevenient grace is also sometimes called enabling grace or pre-regenerating grace. This is God's unmerited favor toward totally depraved people, who are unworthy of God's blessing and unable to seek God or

---

31 Ben Henshaw. "The Arminian and Calvinist Ordo Salutis: A Brief comparative Study." Accessed online on 11/14/2017, http://evangelicalarminians.org/the-arminian-and-calvinist-ordo-salutis-a-brief-comparative-study.

trust in him in and of themselves.... It is the grace that, among other things, frees our wills to believe in Christ and his gospel.[32]

Man's ability to respond to this "prevenient grace" is of major importance to Arminian theology. Arminian theologian F. Leroy Forlines elaborates,

> If descendants of Adam do not in some sense have freedom of will, they have lost their personhood. One of the factors involved in being a person is to have power of choice or the ability to will. The will can choose and act only to the extent that it is free. To deprive the will of freedom is to deprive it of being a will. I think the debate between Calvinism and Arminianism should be framed over whether fallen man is a functioning, personal being. Does he have a functioning mind, heart, and will?[33]

Florines believes the real issue in the Calvinist-Arminian debate is the personhood of man. He continues,

> In my opinion, it has been a mistake over the centuries to focus the conflict between Calvinists and Arminians on whether fallen or redeemed man has a *free will*. The real question is: Is fallen man a personal being, or is he sub-personal? (The same question can also be asked concerning redeemed man.) Does God deal with fallen man as a person? If He does, He deals with him as one who thinks, feels, and acts. To do otherwise undercuts the

---

32 Brian Abasciano, "The FACTS of Salvation: A Summary of Arminian Theology/the Biblical Doctrines of Grace." Accessed online on 11/14/207, http://evangelicalarminians.org/wp-content/uploads/2013/10/Abasciano.-The-FACTS-of-Salvation1.pdf.

33 F Leroy Forlines, *Classical Arminianism: A Theology of Salvation* (Nashville, Tenn: Randall House, 2011), 20-21.

personhood of man.... God designed the relationship to be a relationship between personal beings. Human beings are *personal beings* by God's design and were made for a *personal relationship* with a personal God.[34]

For the Arminian, the Reformed *ordo salutis,* in which God elects in eternity past some men for eternal life and others for eternal damnation, destroys the personhood of man and makes him a pawn in the hand of God. The Arminian understanding of election and predestination, which they do not include in their *ordo salutis,* is based upon union with Christ. Concerning election, Henshaw writes, "We would become the elect of God upon our union with Christ (the Elect One) as we would come to share in His election through union and identification with Him. Faith joins us to Christ...and all the spiritual blessings that reside in Christ become the believer's upon union with Him (Eph 1:3-12)."[35] Regarding predestination, Henshaw writes, "Predestination would have reference to the predetermined destiny of believers through union with Christ. Believers have been predestinated to ultimate adoption and conformity to the image of Christ (glorification). Predestination does not have reference to God's predetermination of certain sinners to become believers and be ultimately saved."[36]

In summary, the Reformed *ordo salutis* elevates the sovereignty of God and begins with God electing, without any reference to man's response, some to receive the gift of life and others to be sentenced to eternal death. The Arminian *ordo salutis* elevates the personhood of man in the image of God and begins with a prevenient grace that is offered to all men. Each person has the ability to respond or not respond in faith to the grace given and is thus held responsible if he does not believe. Needless to say, one's understanding of an *ordo salutis* directly

---

34 Forlines, *Classical Arminianism,* 48-49.
35 Henshaw, "The Arminian and Calvinist Ordo Salutis."
36 Ibid.

affects his soteriology and his progressive sanctification. Theologians explain faith, regeneration, perseverance, and assurance in light of the theology that emerges from their perceived *ordo salutis*. Calvinists view these subjects through deterministic glasses, while Arminians elevate the role of man in the process.

Free Grace theology offers a mediate position. Most Free Grace theologians do not recognize the hard determinism of Calvinism and would agree with the Arminian position that faith precedes regeneration. However, Free Grace theologians separate justification and sanctification and do not see sanctification as a test of eternal life. As a result, they conclude a believer may have full assurance based on his simple belief in the Person and work of Jesus Christ. In Free Grace theology, the *ordo salutis* guarantees that the one who believes in Jesus Christ is eternally saved and secure. Anderson writes,

> For both the Arminians and the Calvinists, one must persevere faithfully until the end of his life or he does not go to heaven. The Arminians claim that the one who does not remain faithful loses his salvation, while the Calvinists claim that one who does not remain faithful, never had salvation. In either case, faithfulness until the end of one's life is the ultimate litmus test for one to spend eternity with God. By making a faithful life a requirement for salvation, teachers of free grace claim that works have been appended to faith, turning God's so great salvation into more of a bribe than a gift. It turns the Christian life into a "have to" life rather than a "thank you" life, which is often the difference between a job and a joy… Only through free grace theology can one legitimately have the assurance of one's salvation in this life and the peace and joy which accompany such assurance.[37]

---

37 Anderson, *Free Grace Soteriology*, ix.

I have only scratched the surface of what has been a centuries long debate, but I thought it necessary to delve somewhat into the theological systems to help understand the differences. I choose to take the verses that speak of a universal atonement at face value. The death Christ died paid for the sin of all mankind, and it must be appropriated by simple faith in Him. (For a list of authors on both sides of these issues, see Appendix A.)

Instructing us to deny ungodliness and worldly desires...

CHAPTER 6:

DENYING UNGODLINESS AND WORLDLY DESIRES

To this point, we have focused on *salvation* as it relates to our eternal destiny. But we must remember that salvation in the Bible is understood from three perspectives. We are justified, saved from the penalty of sin, the moment we believe. We also begin our Christian walk the moment we believe; we call this sanctification. We are progressively being delivered from the power of sin in our daily walk. Ultimately, one day, we will be saved from the very presence of sin when we die or when we are raptured and we go to be with the Lord, and we call this glorification. Our focus now will shift to how grace instructs or teaches us.

In Romans 5:1-2, we see justification and sanctification being by faith through grace, *"Therefore, having been justified by faith, we have peace with God through our Lord Jesus Christ"* (Rom 5:1). It is our justification that puts us in the position to now grow in God's grace. Romans 5:2 continues, *"through whom also we have obtained our introduction by faith into this grace in which we stand; and we exult in hope of the glory of God."* It is through Jesus that we are both justified and sanctified. Just as justification is by faith through grace, so also is our sanctification by faith through grace.

Paul tells Titus, "The grace of God has appeared...*instructing us...*" Some people think that teaching grace will cause people to abuse it and live sinful lives. However, the Bible clearly teaches that grace understood properly leads to godly living. Paul tells Titus that grace instructs us to deny ungodliness and worldly desires. What are *ungodliness* and *worldly desires*?

Although many people think that ungodliness refers to acts that are wicked, evil, dishonest, etc., truth is, much that is highly moral is also ungodly. Harper's Bible Dictionary says this about ungodliness, "Basically, the godless or ungodly person is one who lives, acts, and thinks as though God could be ignored or spurned."[1] Therefore, anything that an unsaved person or a believer does without taking God into account can be considered ungodliness. Because God is our creator (believer and unbeliever) and also our Father (believers), the only proper attitude should be one of absolute dependence upon Him in all things. J.F. Strombeck rightly observes that from Adam on, our tendency is to depend on ourselves instead of God. He writes, "The history of man from Adam to the present day is a history of dependence upon self and independence of God. He has been largely left out of man's thinking. Man has planned, acted, and lived as though God did not exist. All this is ungodliness."[2]

Ungodliness in the life of the believer is anything, thought or deed, that leaves God out of the picture. Paul tells Timothy that ungodliness

---

1 P. J. Achtemeier, Harper & Row, P., & Society of Biblical Literature. 1985. *Harper's Bible dictionary*. Includes index. (1st ed.). Harper & Row: San Francisco.

2 J.F. Strombeck, *Disciplined By Grace* (Strombeck Foundation, Moline, Ill. 1975 Edition), 32.

is strengthened by worldly things (2 Tim 2:16) which brings us to the second area we are told to deny: *worldly desires.*

Strong's Concordance defines the word for desire as, "desire, craving, longing, desire for what is forbidden, lust."[3] Worldly desires would then be any desire, craving, lusting, or longing for what the world system has to offer. Concerning the world, New Testament Greek scholar K.S. Wuest says,

> 'World' is aiōn (αιων) which Trench defines as "that floating mass of thoughts, opinions, maxims, speculations, hopes, impulses, aims, aspirations, at any time current in the world, which it may be impossible to seize and accurately define, but which constitute a most real and effective power, being the moral or immoral atmosphere which at every moment of our lives we inhale, again inevitably to exhale." Christians live in this atmosphere. We breathe it. It confronts us wherever we go. It seeks our destruction. It is pernicious. It surrounds us like the air we breathe. We take it in unconsciously like every breath of air we breathe.[4]

Scripture is very clear that friendship with the world is in direct conflict with our relationship with God.

> *"You adulteresses, do you no know that friendship with the world is hostility toward God? Therefore, whoever wishes to be a friend of the world makes himself an enemy of God." (Jas 4:4)*

> *"For all that is in the world, the lust of the flesh and the lust of the eyes and the boastful pride of life, is not from the Father, but is from the world." (1 Jn 2:16)*

---

3 Strong, J. 1996. *The exhaustive concordance of the Bible : Showing every word of the test of the common English version of the canonical books, and every occurrence of each word in regular order.* (electronic ed.). Woodside Bible Fellowship: Ontario.

4 Wuest, K. S. 1997, c1984. *Wuest's word studies from the Greek New Testament : For the English reader .* Eerdmans: Grand Rapids.

"See to it that no one takes you captive through philosophy and empty deception, according to the tradition of men, according to the elementary principles of the world, rather than according to Christ." (Col 2:8)

Jesus warns in the Parable of the Sower that the world can choke out the effectiveness of the Word in our lives.

"And others are the ones on whom the seed was sown among the thorns; these are the ones who have heard the word, and the worries of the world, and the deceitfulness of riches, and the desires for other things enter in and choke the word, and it becomes unfruitful." (Mk 4:18-19)

The unbeliever who lives a worldly life is only living by his or her nature. The believer who walks by the Spirit is living by his or her true nature. The conflict arises when the believer lives a life that is contrary to his or her true nature. This is a recipe for disaster and explains why so many Christians are living defeated lives void of a close relationship with God. Chambers describes this state well:

To be "a friend of the world" means that we take the world as it is and are perfectly delighted with it—the world is all right and we are very happy in it. Never have the idea that the worldling is unhappy; he is perfectly happy, as thoroughly happy as a Christian. The people who are unhappy are the worldlings or the Christians if they are not at one with the principle which unites them. If a worldling is not a worldling at heart, he is miserable; and if a Christian is not a Christian at heart he carries his Christianity like a headache instead of something worth having, and not being able to get rid of his head, he cannot get rid of his headache.[5]

---

5 O. Chambers 1996, c1947. *Biblical ethics*. Marshall, Morgan & Scott: Hants UK.

How do we measure or evaluate our lives in relation to ungodliness and worldly desires? The Word of God provides lists for the believer to serve as guides by which he or she can know if ungodliness and worldly desires are being manifested. The book of Galatians provides a foundational principle of how we are to serve the Lord: *"But I say,* walk by the Spirit, and you will not *carry out the desire of the flesh"* (Gal 5:16). The implication is quite clear: If the believer chooses to not walk by the Spirit, he can anticipate carrying out the desire of the flesh. This can be seen from two perspectives:

1. Legalism (which looks good on the outside, but will inevitably eliminate the grace walk with God—it is human good which in effect is NO GOOD).

2. Licentiousness (the flesh expression in sin, inside and outside).

> *"Now the deeds of the flesh are evident, which are: immorality, impurity, sensuality, idolatry, sorcery, enmities, strife, jealousy, outbursts of anger, disputes, dissensions, factions, envying, drunkenness, carousing, and things like these..."* (Gal 5:19-21)

Ephesians 4 and 5 provide a second listing. Here are some excerpts:

> *"Let all bitterness and wrath and clamor and slander be put away from you, along with all malice...do not let immorality or any impurity or greed even be named among you...and there must be no filthiness and silly talk, or coarse jesting... And do not participate in the unfruitful deeds of darkness... for it is disgraceful even to speak of the things which are done by them in secret... And do not get drunk with wine, for that is dissipation..."*

Colossians 3:5-9 provides yet another listing:

> *"Therefore consider the members of your earthly body as dead to immorality, impurity, passion, evil desire, and*

greed, which amounts to idolatry... But now you also, put them all aside: anger, wrath, malice, slander, and abusive speech from your mouth. Do not lie to one another..."

Even though the accusation is raised that teaching grace promotes ungodliness and worldly living, the opposite is actually true. Paul is very clear that it is grace that instructs us to deny ungodliness and worldly desires. The book of Titus teaches the proper understanding of grace. Grace, correctly understood, does not teach the believer to live according to the flesh, but on the contrary, grace teaches a positive approach to life—one of Holy Spirit control (to live sensibly, righteously, and godly—our next chapter). Paul answers the question of license to sin in Romans 6:1-2,

"What shall we say then? Are we to continue in sin that grace might increase? May it never be! How shall we who died to sin still live in it?"

Scripture is clear that grace DOES NOT teach sinful living. But if grace is not rules or law or lists of things to do or not do, how does grace instruct us? Read carefully the words of Strombeck:

The discipline of grace brings to mind and soul the goodness and beauty of God. His unfailing love, and His all-inclusive provision. When the heart sees this goodness of God and the riches of His grace; the pleasures, preferment, honor and wealth of the world lose their glamour. They are seen as temporal in contrast to the eternal values of God. The believer who realizes that through grace, and grace alone, he has been saved out of the lost and condemned world unto an indescribably glorious eternity with God sets his affection on things above – not on things on this earth. It is the work of grace to create and sustain this attitude.

Ethics can teach men to deny the dishonest, immoral, and debased things of this world; but grace alone can teach the believer to deny himself the beautiful, attractive, and pleasant things with which God is not identified.

By grace the believer has been called out of the ungodly world and delivered from the condemnation resting upon it. By grace he is also delivered from the desire for the things of the world, and his desires become centered in Christ and things of Him.

The teachings of grace do not compromise with the world nor permit careless living. Unfortunately, some hold that there is a Christian liberty which permits participation in worldly pleasures. That is not liberty, it is license and is entirely at variance with the teachings of grace that worldly lusts should be denied. True Christian liberty is deliverance from the law of sin in the body with its desires for the pleasures of the world.[6]

To be instructed by grace is to understand our standing—secure in Christ by grace alone, through faith alone, and our state—freedom to live the Christian life by the power of the indwelling Holy Spirit. Our perspective shifts from what the world has to offer and our desires for those things to God and our relationship with Him. The questions are no longer, "What can I do, or what can I get away with?" but "How can I please my Lord?" Godly living results from a relationship and walk with God rather than rules and regulations! We will see in the next chapter that there are disciplines like prayer, Bible study, and fellowship with other believers that promote godliness, but these disciplines have to be by the power of the Spirit. Otherwise, they will simply become a set of regulations that we think will produce spirituality.

---

6 J.F. Strombeck, *Disciplined By Grace* (Strombeck Foundation, Moline, Ill. 1975 Edition), 34.

And to live sensibly, righteously and godly in the present age...

CHAPTER 7:

LIVING SENSIBLY, RIGHTEOUSLY AND GODLY IN THIS PRESENT AGE

We saw that grace teaches us to deny ungodliness and worldly desires. Paul continues in Titus 2:12, *"For the grace of God has appeared...instructing us...to live **sensibly, righteously and godly** in the present age."* The grace of God teaches the believer how to live from two perspectives. We have seen the negative side, or the things we take away, in that we are to deny ungodliness and worldly desires. We now look at the positive side, or the things we add. God's grace teaches us to live sensibly, righteously, and godly. Romans 6 is clear that in Christ, we no longer have to live ungodly lives or pursue worldly desires. Having been set free because of Christ's crucifixion, the "flesh" has no more authority or power that it might reign over us. The believer no longer is made to sin—it is a choice. The old man has been rendered without power. We saw in our last lesson that the flesh can produce both sin and human good. In contrast to the flesh, the indwelling Spirit of God empowers the believer to not only stay away from sin, but the capability to produce divine or spiritual good. Titus 2 exhorts us to live **sensibly, righteously**, and **godly**.

It is important to understand that living sensibly, righteously, and godly is not automatic. There are choices that we have to make. The verb "to live" is in the Greek subjunctive mood, the mood of potential (might live). This indicates that it is not automatic but is potentially ours by making correct choices. Let's look first at *living sensibly*.

The Greek word translated "sensibly" is *sōphronōs,* which occurs only here in this form. It is a derivative of the word *sōphrōn* which Strong defines as, "...of a sound mind, sane, in one's senses... curbing one's desires and impulses, self-controlled, temperate."[1] We see this same word used in Titus 1:8 in relation to elders, in 2:2 to older men, in 2:4 to older women, in 2:5 to young women, and in 2:6 to young men. It is to be understood as living life level-headed or thinking clearly.

In contrast to one who is sensible would be the "double-minded man" of James 1:8 who is "unstable in all his ways." It is interesting that just a few verses before, James instructs us:

> "...*if any of you lacks wisdom, let him ask of God, who gives to all men generously and without reproach, and it will be given to him.*" (Jas 1:5)

There is a correlation then between being sensible and living life wisely. Knowledge of the Scripture is crucial if we are to live life wisely and sensibly:

> "*The testimony of the Lord is sure, making wise the simple.*" (Ps 19:7b)

---

1 Strong, J. 1996. *The exhaustive concordance of the Bible: Showing every word of the test of the common English version of the canonical books, and every occurrence of each word in regular order.* (electronic ed.). Woodside Bible Fellowship.: Ontario.

"Therefore be careful how you walk, not as unwise men, but as wise, making the most of your time, because the days are evil. So then do not be foolish, but understand what the will of the Lord is." (Eph 5:15-17)

To live sensibly is not something that we can do in and of ourselves. Those who live sensibly and walk wisely must do so by the power of the indwelling Holy Spirit. As we yield ourselves to God's Spirit, we put ourselves in position to understand and live life in a way that is pleasing to Him.

The second mode of living taught by grace is righteous living. The word translated righteously is *dikaios*. It means "(1) just, agreeably to right; (2) properly, as is right; (3) uprightly."[2] It indicates that the believer's life is to line up with the character of God if, in fact, he or she represents the very person of Christ. Where the word sensible speaks of *thinking clearly*, this word speaks of *living consistently*. This word is used five times in the New Testament: Luke 23:41, 1 Corinthians 15:34, 1 Thessalonians 2:10, Titus 2:12, and 1 Peter 2:23. Notice the context of blameless behavior in 1 Thessalonians 2:10:

"You are witnesses, and so is God, how devoutly and uprightly (diakaios) and blamelessly we behaved toward you believers."

In 1 Peter 2:23, this word characterizes God's judgments. It should be obvious that a life that is lived *righteously* will be one of Christlikeness that can be produced only by the indwelling Holy Spirit. In Romans 6, Paul sets forth the truths of living by the power of the *new man*, that is, walking in newness of life, as opposed to living under the influence and power of the *old man*. In verse 6, we are told that the old self was crucified with Christ. Verse 11 tells us that we must *reckon* or *consider*

---

2 Strong, *Exhaustive Concordance* (electronic ed.).

this fact to be true so that sin cannot have dominion or reign over us. The point is that we do not have to sin! Sin is no longer our master. We can live righteously by presenting ourselves to God and not to the old man, the sin nature. Notice Paul's words in verse 16:

> "Do you not know that when you present yourselves to someone as slaves for obedience, you are slaves of the one whom you obey, either of sin resulting in death, or of obedience resulting in righteousness?"

In Romans 8, Paul makes it clear that it is the Spirit within us that sets us free from the law of sin and death.

The third way grace instructs us is in the area of godly living. The word translated godly is *eusebos*. It can be understood as pious or expressing piety or godliness[3]. This, of course, is in the positive sense. When we hear of someone acting pious, we immediately think of pride in the person's claim. In this passage, we see the person who would be characterized as godly. This speaks of his or her overall character. Of course, godliness would be Christlikeness. Often, Paul tells us to *put on* certain things. The word translated "put on" is *enduo* (ἐνδύω) which means "to sink into (clothing), put on, clothe one's self."[4] In Romans 13:12, we are told to "put on" the armor of light and in verse 14, we are told to *"put on the Lord Jesus Christ, and make no provision for the flesh in regard to its lusts."* When we clothe ourselves with the person of Christ and are in fellowship with Him, then our lives will be godly. In Ephesians 4:22-24, we are told to lay aside the old self and put on the new self *"...which in the likeness of God has been created in righteousness and holiness of the truth."* Godly living is a result of walking in the Spirit which means that our new man, our new creation in Christ, is in control. Our yielded-ness becomes the issue. We can yield to the flesh and reap

---

3 Strong, *Exhaustive Concordance* (electronic ed.).
4 Ibid.

the corruption it brings, or we can yield to the Holy Spirit and reap the harvest of sensible, righteous, and godly living.

Below is the summary of the meanings of *sensibly, righteously,* and *godly*:

For the grace of God has appeared... instructing us... to live sensibly, righteously and godly...

Sensibly	*sophronos*	of sound mind, sane curbing desires/ impulses self-controlled	Ti 1:8, 2:2, 2:4, 2:5, 2:6
Righteously	*dikaios*	Just, agreeably to right, properly, as is right, uprightly.	Lk 23:41, 1 Cor 15:34, 1 Thess 2:10, 1 Pet 2:23
Godly	*eusebos*	Pious, piety, godliness, Christ likeness	2 Tim 3:12

Our Christian life is often described in the Bible by the word "walk." How we should walk is the subject of the next chapter.

And to live sensibly, righteously and godly in the present age...

CHAPTER 8:

WALKING WORTHY OF OUR CALLING

*"I, therefore, the prisoner of the Lord, entreat you to **walk in a manner worthy of the calling with which you have been called.**"*

Ephesians 4:1

O f the 387 times the word *walk* or *walked* is used in the Old Testament, 277 of the usages are translated from the Hebrew word *halak*. Strong's lexicon defines this word as, "1 to go, walk, come. 1A (Qal). 1A1 to go, walk, come, depart, proceed, move, go away. 1A2 to die, live, manner of life (fig.)." [1] The latter definition of "live" or "manner of life" is seen often. Notice that both Enoch and Noah were men who walked with God:

*"Then Enoch **walked with God** three hundred years after he became the father of Methuselah, and he had other sons and*

---

1 Strong, J. 1996. *The exhaustive concordance of the Bible : Showing every word of the test of the common English version of the canonical books, and every occurrence of each word in regular order.* (electronic ed.). Woodside Bible Fellowship : Ontario.

*daughters. So all the days of Enoch were three hundred and sixty-five years. **Enoch walked with God**; and he was not, for God took him."* (Gen 5:22-24)

*"These are the records of the generations of Noah. Noah was a righteous man, blameless in his time; **Noah walked with God**."* (Gen 6:9)

We are often encouraged to walk *in* something, meaning that we live our lives in accordance to that thing.

"Teach me Your way, O Lord; I will walk in Your truth; Unite my heart to fear Your name. (Ps 86:11)

"Teach me the way in which I should walk; For to You I lift up my soul." (Ps 143:8)

This idea of our "walk" being our manner of life, or how we live our life, is carried over into the New Testament by the use of the Greek word *peripateo*, which means, "1 to walk. 1A to make one's way, progress; to make due use of opportunities. 1B Hebrew for, to live. 1B1 to regulate one's life. 1B2 to conduct one's self. 1B3 to pass one's life."[2]

We will see that the "walk" passages all relate to how we live our lives on a daily, moment by moment basis. This walk can be seen both negatively, ways that we should not walk, and a positively, ways in which we should walk.

1. Walk: (in a negative sense)

- Not according to the flesh

"...in order that the requirement of the Law might be fulfilled in us, who do not walk according to the flesh, but according to the Spirit." (Rom 8:4; cf. 2 Cor 10:2)

---

2 Strong, *Exhaustive Concordance* (electronic ed.).

- Not in craftiness

  "...but we have renounced the things hidden because of shame, not walking in craftiness or adulterating the word of God..." (2 Cor 4:2a)

- Not in sins

  "And you were dead in your trespasses and sins, in which you formerly walked..." (Eph 2:1-2)

- Not as Gentiles

  "...walk no longer just as the Gentiles also walk, in the futility of their mind..." (Eph 4:17)

- Not in the darkness

  "If we say that we have fellowship with Him and yet walk in the darkness, we lie and *do not practice the truth."* (1 Jn 1:6)

2. Walk: (in a positive sense)

- In newness of life

  "Therefore we have been buried with Him through baptism into death, in order that as Christ was raised from the dead through the glory of the Father, so we too might walk in newness of life." (Rom 6:4)

- According to love

  "...and walk in love, just as Christ also loved you, and gave Himself up for us, an offering and a sacrifice to God as a fragrant aroma." (Eph 5:2; cf. Rom 14:15)

- By faith

  "...for we walk by faith, not by sight..." (2 Cor 5:7)

- By the Spirit

  "But I say, walk by the Spirit and you will not carry out the desire of the flesh... If we live by the Spirit, let us also walk by the Spirit. (Gal 5:16, 25)

- In good works

  "For we are His workmanship, created in Christ Jesus for good works, which God prepared beforehand, that we should walk in them." (Eph 2:10)

- As children of light

  "...for you were formerly darkness, but now you are light in the Lord; walk as children of light..." (Eph 5:8)

- In the light

  "...but if we walk in the light as He Himself is in the light, we have fellowship with one another, and the blood of Jesus His Son cleanses us from all sin." (1 Jn 1:7)

- As wise men

  "Therefore be careful how you walk, not as unwise men, but as wise." (Eph 5:15)

- In a manner worthy of the Lord

  "...that you may be filled with the knowledge of His will in all spiritual wisdom and understanding, so that you may walk in a manner worthy of the Lord, to please Him in all respects..." (Col 1:9-10)

- In Christ

  "As you therefore have received Christ Jesus the Lord, so walk in Him." (Col 2:6)

- According to His commandments

  "And this is love, that we walk according to His commandments. This is the commandment, just as you have heard from the beginning, that you should walk in it." (2 Jn 6)

- In truth

  "For I was very glad when brethren came and bore witness to your truth, that is, how you are walking in truth. I have no greater joy than this, to hear of my children walking in the truth." (3 Jn 3-4)

- Worthy of our calling

  "I, therefore, the prisoner of the Lord, entreat you to walk in a manner worthy of the calling with which you have been called." (Eph 4:1)

It is clear that the life of a believer is categorized by the word "walk." C. Sumner Wemp, Bible college president and author of *How On Earth Can I Be Spiritual*, writes of three walks that the believer should experience:

1. With God. That is our *purpose!*

   "...Noah was a righteous man, blameless in his time; Noah walked with God." (Gen 6:9b)

2. After Christ. That is our *pattern!*

   "And He said to them, "Follow Me, and I will make you fishers of men." (Matt 4:19)

3. In the Spirit. That is our *power!*

   "...walk by the Spirit and you will not carry out the desire of the flesh." (Gal 5:16)[3]

---

3 Sumner C. Wemp, *How On Earth Can I Be Spiritual?* (Thomas Nelson Inc., Publishers, Nashville, New York, 1978), 61.

Indeed, it is by walking in the Spirit that we have the power to fulfill all the other walks. It is by walking in the Spirit that we can overcome the emotional ups and downs and develop a walk that is consistent. To walk in the Spirit means to walk in dependence on the Spirit. It is interesting that Paul tells us that we will not *"carry out the desires of the flesh."* He does not say that we will never be tempted or have desires to sin. Temptation is not sin. It is the yielding to temptation, the fulfilling of that desire, that is sin. It is crucial that when temptations come that we consciously rely on the Spirit. When we do fail, it is just as important that we immediately confess the sin and continue in our walk. Every believer should know 1 John 1:9 by heart:

> *"If we confess our sins, He is faithful and righteous to forgive us our sins and to cleanse us from all unrighteousness."*

It is by moment-by-moment dependence upon the Holy Spirit and confession when we do fail that we have the power to walk in the Spirit. This 'Spirit walk' will produce in us all the things that make our walk "worthy of His calling"!

Looking for the blessed hope and the appearing of the glory of our great God and Savior, Christ Jesus...

CHAPTER 9:

LOOKING FOR THE BLESSED HOPE AND APPEARING

Jesus is coming back! His return to set up His millennial kingdom is prophesized throughout Scripture. However, there is disagreement among believers as to when His return will be. Is Jesus coming back only once for a final judgment or does he come for His church prior to His return to the earth? Eschatology, the doctrine of last things, deals with future events and two main interpretations have been offered. To lay the groundwork, we must first think about a biblical philosophy of history.

A biblical philosophy of history deals with the issue of meaning. "It offers a systematic interpretation of history. It covers the entire scope of history...including the *what* and *why* of the future."[1] Author and

---

1 Renald E. Showers, *There Really Is A Difference: A Comparison of Covenant and Dispensational Theology* (Bellmawr, NJ, 1990), 2.

Bible teacher Renald Showers lists six necessary elements of a biblical philosophy of history:

> First *it must contain an ultimate purpose or goal for history toward the fulfillment of which all history moves.* Second, *it must recognize distinctions or things that differ in history...* third...*it must have a proper concept of the progress of revelation...fourth...it must have a unifying principle which ties the distinctions and the progressive stages of revelation together and directs them toward the fulfillment of the purpose of history...*Fifth, *it must give a valid explanation of why things have happened the way they have, why things are the way they are today, and where things are going in the future...* Sixth, *it must offer appropriate answers to man's three basic questions: Where have we come from? Why are we here? Where are we going?*[2]

Since the time of the Reformation, two primary systems have emerged that try to outline a biblical philosophy of history. They have developed into what we now call Covenant Theology and Dispensational Theology. "Covenant Theology attempts to develop the Bible's philosophy of history on the basis of covenants."[3] Some Covenant Theologians see two covenants, Works and Grace, and others see three, adding Redemption, as "governing categories for the understanding of the entire Bible."[4] Another author and professor of theology, Michael Vlach, writes, "It is a system of theology that views God's eternal plan of salvation through the outworking of three covenants – the Covenant of Works, Covenant of Grace, and Covenant of Redemption."[5] Covenant

---

2 Showers, *There Really A Difference*, 2-6.
3 Ibid., 8.
4 Charles C. Ryrie, *Dispensationalism* (Chicago: Moody Publishers, 2007), 214.
5 Michael J. Vlach, "New Covenant Theology Compared With Covenantalism." *The Masters Seminary Journal* 18 no 1 (Fall 2007): 202.

Theology (hereafter CT), has strong ties to Reformed Theology which emphasizes continuity between the Old and New Testaments. Covenant Theologian Michael Horton states, "Reformed theology is synonymous with covenant theology."[6] He expands by saying, "whenever Reformed theologians attempt to explore and explain the riches of Scripture, they are always thinking covenantally about every topic they take up."[7]

Several theological distinctions accompany CT. One is a hermeneutic that interprets the Old Testament through the lens of the New Testament. Because of the idea of one redeemed community, the church becomes the recipient of the specific Old Testament promises made to Israel. CT negates the literal rule promised to David's seed in the Davidic Covenant (2 Sam 7:12-17) and the land promises made to Israel in the Land or Palestinian Covenant (Deut 29:1 – 30:20). In light of this, there will be no millennial rule of Christ on earth and the promised kingdom becomes a spiritual kingdom in the hearts of men. The New Covenant (Jer 31:31-34) which is made with the house of Israel and the house of Judah is now fulfilled by spiritual Israel, the church. This view is clearly seen in the statements of Berkhof:

> It is very doubtful, however, whether Scripture warrants the expectation that Israel will finally be re-established as a nation, and will as a nation turn to the Lord. Some Old Testament prophecies seem to predict this, but these should be read in the light of the New Testament. Does the New Testament justify the expectation of a future restoration and conversion of Israel as a nation? It is not taught nor even necessarily implied in such passages as Matt. 19:28, and Luke 21:24, which are often quoted in its favor.[8]

---

6 Michael Horton, *Introducing Covenant Theology* (Grand Rapids: Baker Books, 2009), 11.

7 Ibid., 14.

8 L. Berkhof, *Systematic Theology* (Grand Rapids, MI: Wm. B. Eerdmans Publishing Co., 1938), 699.

In summary, CT teaches a strong continuity between the Old Testament and the New Testament based on two or three covenants that are the basis of interpretation. CT uses a hermeneutic that reads the New Testament back into the Old Testament so that the specific promises to Israel as a nation are now fulfilled by the church or will be fulfilled in the new creation. There will be no literal millennial kingdom on earth and the Mosaic Law, at least the moral aspect, is still applicable for the church today. As infants were brought into the community of faith under the Law by circumcision, now infants should be brought into the new Israel, the church, by baptism. CT strongly upholds the continuity of the Bible. Dispensational Theology, on the other hand, sees many areas of discontinuity in the Bible. A brief look at Dispensational Theology will further set the stage to understanding *"the blessed hope and appearing of Jesus."*

Rather than seeing two or three theological covenants as the basis of biblical interpretation, Dispensational Theology (hereafter DT) sees the Bible unfolding through different dispensations or economies that are progressive through biblical revelation. Charles Ryrie defines a dispensation as "a distinguishable economy in the outworking of God's purpose."[9] "Dispensationalists arrive at their system of interpretation through two primary principles: (1) maintaining a consistently literal method of interpretation, and (2) maintaining a distinction between Israel and the church."[10] Covenant theologians often make the claim that DT is a recent theology and thus should not be taken seriously.[11] They claim that DT began with John Nelson Darby (1800-1882). However, Paul Enns, theologian and writer, points out that a strong case can be made that "the foundations and initial developments of dispensationalism are ancient."[12] Darby is recognized as "having much

---

9 Charles C. Ryrie, *Dispensationalism Today* (Chicago: Moody Press, 1974), 29.

10 Paul Enns, *The Moody Handbook of Theology* (Chicago: Moody Press, 1989), 513.

11 Ryrie, *Dispensationalism*, 69-86. Ryrie documents this charge and similar ones and defends an earlier origin of Dispensationalism.

12 Enns, *The Moody Handbook*, 513.

to do with the systematizing and promoting of dispensationalism."[13] Several of the church fathers such as Justin Martyr (A.D. 110-200), Irenaeus (A.D. 130-200), and Clement of Alexandria (A.D. 150-220) identified different dispensations.[14] French philosopher Pierre Poiret (1646-1719) "wrote a six volume systematic theology entitled *L'O Economie Divine*. In this modified Calvinistic and premillennial work, Poiret presented a seven-fold dispensational scheme...."[15] Clearly, both CT and DT were formalized into theological systems during the same time period following the Reformation. DT was popularized in the Scofield Reference Bible in the early 1900s and in schools such as Moody Bible Institute, Dallas Theological Seminary, Talbot Seminary, Grace Seminary, Faith Seminary, and Philadelphia College of Bible.[16]

In defining dispensationalism, Ryrie asks the question, "What is the *sine qua non* (the absolutely indispensable part) of the system?"[17] He gives a threefold answer:

1. *A dispensationalist keeps Israel and the church distinct...* This is probably the most basic theological test of whether or not a person is a dispensationalist and is undoubtedly the most practical and conclusive.

2. *This distinction between Israel and the church is born out of a system of hermeneutics that is usually called literal interpretation...* To be sure, literal/historical/grammatical interpretation is not the sole possession or practice of dispensationalists, but the consistent use of it in all areas of biblical interpretation is.

3. A third aspect of the *sine qua non... concerns the underlying purpose of God in the world...* To the normative dispensationalist, the soteriological, or saving, program of God is not the only program but one of the means God is using in the total program

---

13 Ryrie, *Dispensationalism*, 77.
14 Enns, *The Moody Handbook*, 513-514.
15 Ibid.
16 Ibid., 517.
17 Ryrie, *Dispensationalism*, 45.

of glorifying Himself. Scripture is not man-centered as though salvation were the main theme, but it is God-centered because His glory is the center.[18]

Concerning this third area of glorifying God, Elliott Johnson, Dallas Theological Seminary professor and founder of Asian Theological Seminary, writes,

> The value of Dispensationalism features the distinctive view of the believer's life as a steward of God's will in his appointed time in history. However, the ultimate purpose of telling the story is to have God's story move our hearts to worship. For while it is a story of man in history, that story uncovers the glory of God who shares Himself to accomplish His will for His own people who love Him and are called according to His purposes.[19]

In contrast to CT, DT believes the covenant promises of the Old Testament to Israel will be fulfilled literally on the earth during the millennial kingdom. The promises made in the Abrahamic Covenant, the Davidic Covenant, the Palestinian Covenant, and the New Covenant were made to Israel and will be fulfilled by Israel, not the church. The church is seen as a mystery (Eph 3:1-10) that was not revealed in the Old Testament. "Dispensational ecclesiology defines the church as a distinct body of saints in the present age, having its own divine purpose and destiny and differing from the saints of the past or future ages."[20] Dispensationalists do not recognize the three theological covenants of CT: the Covenant of Works, Covenant of Grace, and Covenant of Redemption. DT does not say that the ideas contained in these supposed

---

18 Ryrie, *Dispensationalism,* 46-48.

19 Elliott Johnson, *A Dispensational Biblical Theology* (Allen, TX: Bold Grace Academic, 2016), 4.

20 John F. Walvoord, *The Millennial Kingdom* (Grand Rapids: Zondervan Publishing House, 1959), 224.

covenants are necessarily unscriptural but, as Ryrie points out, "they are ideas that are not systematized, formalized, and stated by Scripture as covenants... the covenant theologian *never* finds in the Bible the terms *covenant of works* and *covenant of grace*."[21]

DT puts a strong emphasis on the literal historical-grammatical interpretation of the biblical covenants. They believe the Abrahamic, the Davidic, the Palestinian, and the New Covenants are unconditional covenants and depend on God's promise and faithfulness alone for fulfillment. While DT recognizes some conditions within these covenants that depend on human responses, the ultimate fulfillment will be brought about to Israel just as God promised.

In summary, DT is founded on a historical-grammatical or literal hermeneutic that does not read the New Testament back into the Old Testament for the purpose of spiritualizing the promises made to Abraham, David, and the nation of Israel. Israel and the church have distinct purposes in the overall plan of God. DT recognizes the discontinuities of Scripture and sees them in the light of God's progressive revelation and ultimate goal of His glory.

Probably the clearest illustration of the difference between CT and DT is the understanding of the relationship of Israel to the church. The key issue is whether or not the Old Testament promises to national Israel are to be fulfilled literally in the future by Israel, or rather has the church become spiritual Israel and thus inherited the promises made to national Israel. CT, because of the continuity of the system, sees the people of God as the same throughout history. Berkhof writes, "The New Testament Church is essentially one with the Church of the old dispensation."[22] Paul Tan, in his book *The Interpretation of Prophecy* notes, "Covenant theologians teach that the Old Testament Israel and the New Testament church are one

---

21 Ryrie, *Dispensationalism*, 220.
22 Berkhof, *Systematic*, 571.

people, one being the continuation and successor of the other."[23] Berkhof writes, "...the Church existed in the old dispensation as well as in the new, and was *essentially* the same in both, in spite of acknowledged institutional and administrative differences."[24] Dispensational theologian Charles Baker expands,

> This is one of the chief tenets of Covenant Theology. Most covenant theologians are A-millennial and must therefore argue that the present dispensation is the final one in which all of the Old Testament promises must find their fulfillment. These promises were made to Israel; hence the Church must be spiritual Israel, since the Church comprises God's people today. Not only must Israel be spiritualized to mean Gentiles, but the physical and material earthly promises must be spiritualized to mean purely spiritual blessings in heaven.[25]

Tan writes, "Concerning the nation Israel, covenant theologians maintain that Israel is now cast aside because she crucified the Messiah and is now no more special to God than any other nation on earth."[26] He continues, "Covenant theologians hand the Old Testament promises over to the church, and leave the threats and curses often found in the same Old Testament texts behind for Israel."[27]

DT sees discontinuity between Israel and the church. John Walvoord, former President of Dallas Theological Seminary, states, "Dispensational ecclesiology defines the church as a distinct body of saints in the present age, having its own divine purpose and destiny and

---

23 Paul Lee Tan, *The Interpretation of Prophecy* (Winona Lake, Indiana: Assurance Publishers, 1974), 247.
24 Berkhof, *Systematic*, 571.
25 Charles F. Baker, *A Dispensational Theology* (Grand Rapids: Grace Bible College Publications, 1971), 526.
26 Tan, *Interpretation*, 249.
27 Ibid., 250.

differing from the saints of the past or future ages."[28] Ryrie calls "...the doctrine of the Church...the touchstone of dispensationalism."[29] DT recognizes that Israel and the church are always kept distinct in the New Testament and Old Testament.

> The book of Acts speaks frequently of the "church" (nineteen times) and "Israel" (twenty times). However, 'church' refers to those believing at Pentecost and beyond; while "Israel" refers to the nation – historically and ethnically. The terms are never used synonymously or interchangeably. The church is never called "spiritual Israel" or "new Israel" in the NT; furthermore, Israel is never called "the church" in the OT.[30]

Concerning the church as the body of Christ (1 Cor 12:27), Ryrie notes,

> It is distinct because of who are included within that body (i.e., Jews and Gentiles as fellow heirs), and it is distinct because of the new relationships of being in Christ and of Christ's indwelling the members of that body. Both of these distinctives are unique with the church and were not known or experienced by God's people in Old Testament times....[31]

DT also notes that the church had its beginning in the New Testament. Enns notes,

> ...an examination of the New Testament indicates the church is a peculiar New Testament entity that had not previously existed. In Matthew 16:18 Jesus declared, "I will

---

28 Walvoord, *Millennial Kingdom*, 224.
29 Ryrie, *Dispensationalism Today*, 132.
30 Richard L. Mayhue, "New Covenant Theology and Futuristic Premillennialism," *The Master's Seminary Journal* 18, no. 2 (September 2007): 230.
31 Ryrie, *Dispensationalism*, 144.

build my church," indicating the building of the church was future. This point is important. It emphasizes that the church was not yet in existence when Jesus spoke these words. He was making a prediction concerning His future building of the church.[32]

Because Israel and the church are seen to be separate entities by DT, the unfilled Old Testament promises to Israel will be fulfilled by Israel in the future. The church age is something new that was not revealed in the Old Testament and the church does not replace Israel. DT sees the discontinuity between Israel and the church and believes that the promises to Israel will be fulfilled literally in the coming millennial kingdom. The church is a new entity that was not revealed in the Old Testament, consisting of Jew and Gentile made one in the body of Christ.

Two main eschatological systems emerged from Dispensational and Covenant theologies. Premillennialism, which teaches that Christ returns before the millennium, is the view most held by dispensationalists. Amillennialism, which teaches that the millennium is spiritual, not literal, is the view held by most covenant theologians.

A typical Amillennial timeline would look like this:

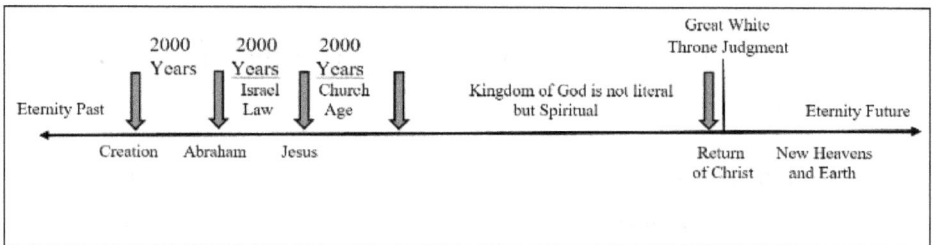

Note that there is no literal 1,000-years kingdom. The kingdom is spiritual and in the hearts of believers. There is only one judgment, the Great White Throne, that occurs at the return of Christ. As

---

32 Enns, *The Moody Handbook*, 348-349.

stated earlier, the problem with an Amillennial view of eschatology is that the Old Testament must be re-interpreted. Judaism clearly understood the promise of a literal kingdom on earth. The phrase, "Behold, days are coming," is used at least five times in Jeremiah when referring to God's future blessings upon Israel (16:14-15; 30:3; 31:31; 31:38; 33:14).

Jeremiah 16:14-15; 30:3 and 33:14-16 specifically tie these blessings to Israel being restored to her land, Jerusalem dwelling in safety, and a "righteous Branch of David" executing justice and righteousness on the earth. Clearly, Jeremiah 31:31-34 is a similar promise to Israel for future restoration and blessings under the New Covenant. Amillennialism teaches that Israel is replaced by the church.

A typical Premillennial timeline would look like this:

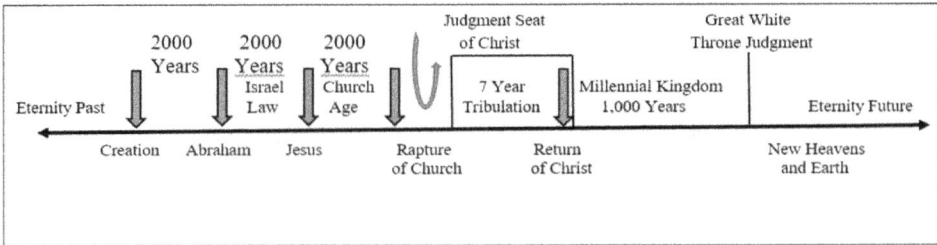

From a premillennial viewpoint, the rapture of the church is the next prophetic event. The Judgment Seat of Christ will occur in heaven during the seven-year tribulation and then the church will return with Christ at the end of the tribulation at His second coming. Believers who survive the tribulation will enter into the 1,000-year millennial kingdom and will be subject to Christ who will rule and reign from Jerusalem. At the end of the millennium. there will be one final rebellion and then the Great White Throne judgment and which Satan and all unbelievers are cast into the lake of fire. Then God will create a new heaven and a new earth, and the new Jerusalem will come down, and God and man will dwell together for eternity.

You may be thinking, "what difference does it make?" Truth is, one's view of the second coming of Christ makes a big difference in how many New Testament texts are understood. If Jesus returns only once at the end of the age, then there will be no rapture of the church, no Judgment Seat of Christ for believers, and no literal millennial kingdom on earth where Christ rules and reigns for 1,000 years. This work is being written from a dispensational viewpoint. The next biblical event in the prophetic timeline will be the rapture of the church. This is the *blessed hope and appearing* that the church-age believer should long for. Indeed, grace teaches us to live in light of the appearing of Christ. Part of living by grace in view of Christ's appearing is to realize that our life on earth counts for eternity and that we will one day have to give an account of lives at the Judgment Seat of Christ—the subject of the next chapter.

Looking for the blessed hope and the appearing of the glory of our great God and Savior, Christ Jesus...

CHAPTER 10:

THE JUDGMENT SEAT OF CHRIST

The eternal destiny of all mankind (individuals) is set while on earth: those who believe in Christ receive eternal life with the Father and those who reject Christ receive eternal separation from the Father. However, Scripture is clear that the works of all individuals, saved and unsaved, will be judged. Hebrews 9:27 says that *"...it is appointed for men to die once and after this comes judgment".* It is critical that we understand the judgments are for *works* and not for *eternal life.* The issue of eternal life is decided while people are still on earth based on their belief or non-belief in Jesus Christ. In terms of *eternity,* ALL SIN was judged in Christ on the cross; therefore, no one goes to hell because they are sinful (everyone is sinful), but because they do not believe in the One who paid in full (redemption) the debt of sin. Yet there are still two judgments seen in Scripture: one for believers and one for unbelievers.

1. The Judgment Seat of Christ

   The works of *the believer* will be judged at the Judgment Seat of Christ, often referred to as the *Bema Seat* after the Greek word βῆμα. Strong's Concordance defines bema as: "2 a raised place mounted by steps. 2A a platform, tribune. 2A1 of the official seat of a judge. 2A2 of the judgment seat of Christ."[1] It is this judgment that we will look at in detail in this chapter. Only believers appear at this judgment. Specifically, the body of Christ, believers from Acts 2 until the Rapture. Scripture is not clear at what point other saints (Old Testament, Tribulation, and Millennial) will receive judgment for their works.

2. The Great White Throne Judgment

   This judgment is described in Revelation 20:11-15 and is specifically for all individuals who have *not believed*. They are at this judgment because their names are not found written in the book of life (v. 15). However, they are judged based on their deeds which are written in other books (vv. 12-13). Only unbelievers appear at this judgment. Neither this judgment nor the Bema Seat are judgments about sin in a judicial sense. Judicially, sin was paid for completely and perfectly by Christ's death on the cross. People will find themselves at the Great White Throne judgment because they did not accept God's perfect provision for their sin, that is, they did not believe in Jesus.

---

1 Strong, J. 1996. *The exhaustive concordance of the Bible : Showing every word of the test of the common English version of the canonical books, and every occurrence of each word in regular order.* (electronic ed.). Woodside Bible Fellowship.: Ontario.

Bing points out differences between the two judgments:[2]

Which Judgment?	Great White Throne	Judgment Seat of Christ
Who is judged?	Only Unbelievers	Only Believers
When is the judgment?	After the Millennium	After the Rapture and before the Marriage Supper of the Lamb
What is the witness?	Books and the Book of Life	Each person gives an account
What is the role of works?	Evidence for condemnation and degree of suffering	Basis for rewards or denial of rewards
What is the final result?	Eternal condemnation	Rewards bestowed or withheld
What is the issue?	Faith in Christ as Savior	Faithfulness to Christ as Lord
What are the main Bible passages?	Dan 12:1-3; Jn 5:22-29; Rev 20:11-15	Rom 14:10; 1 Cor 3:11-15; 4:1-5; 2 Cor 5:10; 2 Tim 4:8

THE JUDGMENT SEAT OF CHRIST

In the New Testament, we have three major passages addressing the Judgment Seat:

1. Romans 14:10-14

   "But why do you judge your brother? Or why do you show contempt for your brother? **For we shall all stand before the judgment seat of Christ.** *For it is written, 'As I live, says the LORD, every knee shall bow to Me, and every tongue shall confess to God.' So then each of us shall give account of himself to God. Therefore let us not judge one another anymore, but rather resolve this, not to put a stumbling block or a cause to fall in our brother's way." (NKJV)*

---

2 Charles Bing *Gracenotes* https://www.gracelife.org/resources/gracenotes/?lang=eng&id=68

2.   2 Corinthians 5:9-11

*"Therefore we make it our aim, whether present or absent, to be well pleasing to Him. **For we must all appear before the judgment seat of Christ,** that each one may receive the things done in the body, according to what he has done, whether good or bad. Knowing, therefore, the terror of the Lord, we persuade men; but we are well known to God, and I also trust are well known in your consciences."* (NKJV)

3.   1 Corinthians 3:10-15

"According to the grace of God which was given to me, as a wise master builder I have laid the foundation, and another builds on it. But let each one take heed how he builds on it. For no other foundation can anyone lay than that which is laid, which is Jesus Christ. Now if anyone builds on this foundation with gold, silver, precious stones, wood, hay, straw, each one's work will become clear; for the Day will declare it, because it will be revealed by fire; and the fire will test each one's work, of what sort it is. If anyone's work which he has built on it endures, he will receive a reward. If anyone's work is burned, he will suffer loss; but he himself will be saved, yet so as through fire." (NKJV)

Although the Judgment Seat is not specifically mentioned in 1 Corinthians 3, the content clearly points to the Bema Seat. Paul, the wise master builder, led these Corinthians to faith in the Lord Jesus, laying the foundation on which all else is built. In time, both Apollos and Peter spent time in Corinth teaching the Corinthians. Paul says that any who teaches must build (building metaphor) carefully using only the best of materials. Believers' works will be tested by fire. The analogy is clear: when the fiery test comes (and it will), only those things done in the power of the Holy Spirit will remain. The issue at the Judgment Seat is reward or loss thereof. The loss is loss of reward, not salvation, for verse 15 is clear that *"...he himself will be saved..."*

Notice that there are two groups of works in this passage: one group that will burn up when tested by fire and another group that will stand the test of the flames. So, what are the works that will remain and be rewarded? D.M. Panton, British pastor and theologian, makes the following comments on this passage:

> The selection of the material lies within the choice of the disciple. *Every disciple has absolute control over the materials with which he builds.* Contending motives sway the choice: popularity, social prestige, wealth, pleasure, love to Christ, fidelity, a sense of truth, the fear of God. What is the precious stone work? *Material that matches the foundation.* There are a thousand voices in the world today: to the wise man there is but One.[3]

The 'what' of the testing, the material that lasts, is Christlikeness—Christ-like character and conduct. In verse 13, Paul states that, *"...the fire itself will test the quality (motivation) of each man's work."* A few verses later in chapter 4 verse 5, he elaborates on this idea of motives,

> *"Therefore do not go on passing judgment before the time, but wait until the Lord comes who will both bring to light the things hidden in the darkness and **disclose the motives of men's hearts;** and then each man's praise will come to him from God."*

Notice some of the attitudes (motives) of the heart that God will reward:

> *"But you, when you pray, go into your room, and when you have shut your door, pray to your Father who is in the secret*

---

3 D.M. Panton, *The Judgment Seat of Christ*, (Shoettle Publishing Co. Inc., Hayesville, NC, 1984), 20.

place; and your Father who sees in secret will reward you openly." (Matt 6:6 NKJV)

"Judge not, and you shall not be judged. Condemn not, and you shall not be condemned. Forgive, and you will be forgiven." (Lk 6:37 NKJV)

"And whoever gives one of these little ones only a cup of cold water in the name of a disciple, assuredly, I say to you, he shall by no means lose his reward." (Matt 10:42 NKJV)

"Do not be deceived, God is not mocked; for whatever a man sows, that he will also reap." (Gal 6:7 NKJV)

Clearly, those things done with improper motives will not be rewarded.

"Beware of practicing your righteousness before men to be noticed by them; otherwise you have no reward with your Father who is in heaven." (Matt 6:1)

Verses 2 to 6 of Matthew 6 go on to illustrate this principle.

An area that often brings to light our motivations is suffering. In other words, a willingness to endure suffering supports the existence of proper motive. Panton says of suffering, "Suffering generally ensures purity in motive. The Lord counterbalances the fear of men, not only with the more tremendous fear of God, but also by the magnitude of His rewards."[4] Jesus tells us in Luke 6:22-23 that persecution for His sake, properly endured, produces great reward in heaven:

*"Blessed are you when men hate you, and ostracize you, and cast insults at you, and spurn your name as evil, for the sake of the Son of Man. Be glad in that day, and leap for joy, for behold, **your reward is great in heaven**; for in the same way their fathers used to treat the prophets."*

---

4 Panton, *The Judgment Seat of Christ*, 6.

Some would say that to teach rewards is to teach a wrong motive for serving Christ. However, Scripture is clear in many passages that God does reward His children for faithful service. Again, Panton is very insightful:

> No wise disciple can afford to neglect so great a mass of Scripture, or to throw away so mighty an incentive to holiness. *Our discovery of this truth at the Judgment Seat will be too late.* Every seed we drop into the soil, every thought and word and act – is banked in God, and will one day spring up in lovely, or alarming, harvest, - *as* we sowed, *what* we sowed, as *much* as we sowed, and *why* we sowed. Therefore 'LOOK TO YOURSELVES, THAT YE LOSE NOT THE THINGS THAT YE HAVE WROUGHT, BUT THAT YE RECEIVE A FULL REWARD' (2 John 8)"[5]

Of course, our love and service for Christ is always motivated by His great love and service for us. The more we focus on the grace of God, the more our hearts will be stirred to faithfully serve Him. Just a glimpse of eternity and the realization that all we do during this short span of mortal life has eternal consequences should move us to lay aside the things that are temporal and perishing and focus on the things that will remain.

> *"Therefore we do not lose heart, but though our outer man is decaying, yet our inner man is being renewed day by day. For momentary, light affliction is producing for us an eternal weight of glory far beyond all comparison, while we look not at the things which are seen, but at the things which are not seen; for the things which are seen are temporal, but the things which are not seen are eternal."* (2 Cor 4:16-18)

---

5 Panton, *The Judgment Seat of Christ*, 7-8.

Looking for the blessed hope and the appearing of the glory of our great God and Savior, Christ Jesus...

CHAPTER 11:

THE MOTIVES OF OUR HEART

We saw in 1 Corinthians 3:13 that our works will be tested at the Judgment Seat of Christ by fire. This verse says that the *"...fire itself will test the quality of each man's work."* Without a doubt, the quality of our work for God is directly related to the motives of our hearts. Only a few verses later in chapter 4 verse 5, Paul makes the statement:

> *"...wait until the Lord comes who will both bring to light the things hidden in the darkness and disclose **the motives of men's hearts**; and then each man's praise will come to him from God."*

We should also remember our Lord's words in Matthew 6:1:

> *"Beware of practicing your righteousness before men to be noticed by them; otherwise you have no reward with your Father who is in heaven."*

Our thoughts, attitudes, and motivation for serving Christ are critically important. Understanding God's grace in this area will help us keep on the right path and present works at the Judgment Seat of Christ that are gold, silver, and precious stones.

GRACE TEACHES HUMILITY

In the same context of 1 Corinthians 4 where we see the motives of our heart mentioned, we find this statement in verse 7:

> "For who regards you as superior? And what do you have that you did not receive? But if you did receive it, why do you boast as if you had not received it?"

A sad part of our fallen nature is our desire to 'be something' before others. This whole area of pride is out of character with God's program of grace. The Corinthians were boasting in themselves, but Paul (with a touch of sarcasm) reminds them that all that they have, they received from God by His grace. He goes on in the rest of the chapter to contrast the life of the apostles with the life of the arrogant, prideful believer. Power and usefulness for God are clearly seen to be related to humility and trust.

> "Now some have become arrogant, as though I were not coming to you. But I will come to you soon, if the Lord wills, and I shall find out, not the words of those who are arrogant, but their power. For the kingdom of God does not consist in words but in power." (1 Cor 4:18-20)

Strombeck states,

> Dependence upon God produces humility in man. Pride and boasting are traits of natural man, and spring from man's dependence upon self and self-sufficiency. Whatever success comes to man tends to feed and nourish his pride. These traits, though not always obvious, are very persistent

and are also evident in the lives of those who are saved. There is a deep rooted desire to be something. If not openly, yet in the heart persists a feeling of self-importance.[1]

Paul had already reminded them in chapter one that it is God who has the power and that His plan often uses people who are weak and foolish (by the world's standards) so that all the glory will go to the Lord.

> *"For consider your calling, brethren, that there were not many wise according to the flesh, not many mighty, not many noble; but God has chosen the foolish things of the world to shame the wise, and God has chosen the weak things of the world to shame the things which are strong, and the base things of the world and the despised, God has chosen, the things that are not, that He might nullify the things that are, **that no man should boast before God.** But by His doing you are in Christ Jesus, who became to us wisdom from God, and righteousness and sanctification, and redemption, that, just as it is written, **'Let Him who boasts, boast in the LORD.'"** (1 Cor 1:26-31)*

Romans 3:27-28 makes it clear that there is no boasting on our part in our justification:

> *"Where then is boasting? It is excluded. By what kind of law? Of works? No, but by a law of faith. For we maintain that a man is justified by faith apart from the works of the Law."*

It is also clear that our Christian life is by grace through faith which also excludes boasting:

> *"But may it never be that I should boast, except in the cross of our Lord Jesus Christ, through which the world has been crucified to me, and I to the world."* (Gal 6:14)

---

1 J.F. Strombeck, *Disciplined By Grace* (Strombeck Foundation, Moline, Ill. 1975 Edition). 61.

If anyone had reason to boast in themselves, it was the Apostle Paul. In 2 Corinthians 10, 11, and 12, Paul vindicates his apostleship. Yet he understands that all his accomplishments are by God's grace:

"And He has said to me, 'My grace is sufficient for you, for power is perfected in weakness.' Most gladly, therefore, I will rather boast about my weaknesses, that the power of Christ may dwell in me. Therefore I am well content with weaknesses, with insults, with distresses, with persecutions, with difficulties, for Christ's sake; for when I am weak, then I am strong." (2 Cor 12:9-10)

In Philippians 3:4-6, Paul gives his fleshly resumé and it was very impressive! However, in verses 7 and 8, he puts earthly, worldly knowledge in proper perspective when he says, *"...I count all things to be loss in view of the surpassing value of knowing Christ Jesus my Lord, for whom I have suffered the loss of all things, and count them but rubbish..."*

The ultimate example of humility prompted from proper motives was the Lord Jesus:

"Have this attitude in yourselves which was also in Christ Jesus, who, although He existed in the form of God, did not regard equality with God a thing to be grasped, but emptied Himself, taking the form of a bond-servant, and being made in the likeness of men. And being found in appearance as a man, He humbled Himself by becoming obedient to the point of death, even death on a cross." (Phil 2:5-8)

Because Jesus knew with certainty who He was and where He was going, He humbled Himself:

"Jesus, knowing that the Father had given all things into His hands, and that He had come forth from God, and was going back to God, rose from supper, and laid aside His

garments; and taking a towel, He girded Himself about. Then He poured water into the basin, and began to wash the disciples' feet..." (Jn 13:3-5)

In the same sense, every believer, because of the certainty of who he is in Christ and the security of that relationship, can relegate the world to its proper place and focus on serving Christ. Strombeck notes,

> In the same measure that one becomes possessed by the knowledge that he has come from the Father and that his eternal destiny is with Him, things of the world fade into insignificance. As pride has its roots in a desire to be something in the world, the devaluation of the things of the world produces humility. Humility, then, is fostered by a deep sense of complete dependence upon God; by a certain realization of the infinitely glorious position in Christ; by the love of God shed abroad in the heart by the Holy Spirit; by a realization of the infinite power of the Father on one's behalf, and by a certain knowledge that one is borne of God and has an eternal destiny in the presence of and in union with the Father and the Son. It is the work of grace, and grace alone, to impart these glorious truths to the soul and thereby teach humility.[2]

GRACE TEACHES DEVOTION TO CHRIST

Scripture is clear that God desires good works in our lives. Ephesians 2:10 tells us that we should walk in good works. However, devotion to Christ is the basis for service and, in comparison, more important. Jesus brings this truth to light so clearly in Luke 10:38-42 in the account of His visit to Martha's home. Martha was busy serving the Lord while her sister Mary was sitting at His feet listening to His word! When

---

2 Strombeck, *Disciplined By Grace*, 67-68.

Martha questioned the Lord about Mary's lack of help, His reply was unexpected: *"Martha, Martha, you are worried and bothered about so many things; but only a few things are necessary, really only one, for Mary has chosen the good part, which shall not be taken away from her."* Strombeck writes,

> These sisters represent two different attitudes that believers may take toward Christ. Both were intensely interested in Jesus, but there was a vast difference in their attitude toward Him. Martha's attitude was to do some material service for Him... Mary, instead of doing something for Him, sat at His feet and received from Him.... Mary desired to receive spiritual things from Him, Martha was so busy in her task of serving Him with temporal things that she had no time to receive the spiritual things He had come to offer her.[3]

Jesus doesn't rebuke Martha for her service, but He does make the point that devotion to Him is more important. When we sit at the feet of Jesus and understand who He is and what He has done and is doing for us, our pride and boasting in self are completely destroyed. In his message to the church at Ephesus revealed to John in Revelation 2:1-7, Jesus commends them for their doctrinal purity and stand for the faith and their perseverance in the faith. However, in verse four He says, *"But I have this against you, that you have left your first love."* Whatever this 'first love' is, love and devotion for the Lord Jesus Christ must be the underlying theme.

So, we see that our motives in serving Christ are more important than the service itself. Service done with wrong motives will not reap eternal reward. Service done with proper motives and humility of heart will reap great reward. Realizing our humanness and tendency toward pride, we must keep our eyes focused on Jesus and realize that every

---

3 Strombeck, *Disciplined By Grace*, 91-92.

gift we have and every ability we use for Him comes from Him by His grace. This balance between serving and devotion is brought into focus in Hebrews 12. We see in verses 1-3 that we are to serve, here stated as *run the race,* but that service must always come from our devotion to Christ, *fixing our eyes on Jesus.*

> *"...let us also lay aside every encumbrance, and the sin which so easily entangles us, and let us run with endurance the race that is set before us, fixing our eyes on Jesus the author and perfecter of faith, who for the joy set before Him endured the cross despising the shame, and has sat down at the right hand of the throne of God. For consider Him who has endured such hostility by sinners against Himself, so that you may not grow weary and lose heart."*

As we have seen, eternal rewards are promised to believers who serve Christ faithfully with proper motives. By keeping our focus on Jesus, the author and perfecter of faith, we will be able to serve with a sincere heart and motives that are focused on glorifying Him.

Who gave Himself for us to redeem us from every lawless deed...

CHAPTER 12:

GRACE AND LAW

"For the Law was given through Moses; grace and truth were realized through Jesus Christ."

John 1:17

Whatever God gives us because of the merit of Christ is always of grace. In fact, it is the very work of Christ on the cross that is the basis of grace!

"And the Law came in that the transgression might increase; but where sin increased, grace abounded all the more, that, as sin reigned in death, even so grace might reign through righteousness to eternal life through Jesus Christ our Lord." (Rom 5:20-21)

Law, which requires human work and effort, is in direct opposition to grace, which is God's unmerited favor.

> *"And if by grace, then it is no longer of works; otherwise grace is no longer grace. But if it is of works, it is no longer grace; otherwise work is no longer work."* (Rom 11:6 NKJV)

The Law was given through Moses, a member of the sinful human race. Grace and truth were given through Jesus Christ, the Son of God. Notice how these two are contrasted in Hebrews 3:1-6:

> *"...consider Jesus...counted worthy of more glory than Moses.... Now Moses was faithful in all His house as a servant, for a testimony of those things which were to be spoken later; but Christ was faithful as a Son over His house...."*

Christ's priesthood is contrasted with the earthly priesthood (the Law) in Hebrews 7:28:

> *"For the Law appoints men as high priests who are weak, but the word of the oath, which came after the Law, appoints a Son, made perfect forever."*

Later in Hebrews 12:18-24, the old covenant (the Law) and the new covenant (the gospel of grace) "...are contrasted by comparing Mt. Sinai, where the Law was given, with Mt. Zion, the spiritual city, eternal in the heavens and symbolic of the gospel of grace."[1]

> *"For you have not come to a mountain that may be touched... But you have come to Mount Zion, and to the city of the living God, the heavenly Jerusalem, and to myriads of angels... and to Jesus, the mediator of a new covenant, and to the sprinkled blood, which speaks better than the blood of Abel."*

---

1 Charles C. Ryrie, *The Ryrie Study Bible*, (Chicago, Moody Press, 1978), 1854.

Abel's blood cried out for judgment (Gen 4:10-12), but Christ's blood secures acceptance before God (Heb 9:11-12, 10:10, 14). Strombeck writes,

> This pre-eminence of Jesus Christ over Moses is indicative of the pre-eminence of grace over law, the only two grounds upon which God deals with man. The pre-eminence of grace over law can then be said to be as the creator over the creature: as of the divine over the sinful human: as the spiritual over the flesh, as of the infinite over the finite, and as that which endures over that which passes away.[2]

Throughout the New Testament, grace and truth stand in stark contrast to the Law. This is seen from two perspectives:

1. Justification – where eternal salvation is by grace alone through faith alone in Christ alone.
2. Sanctification – where the believer lives not by Law but by the power of the indwelling Holy Spirit.

JUSTIFICATION: ETERNAL LIFE BY GRACE, NOT LAW

Justification by grace through faith in Jesus Christ is covered in detail in chapters one through three. Here, we will simply look at a few of the many Scriptures contrasting salvation by faith with trying to obtain it by the Law. Remember, under Law, man tries to reach up to heaven; under grace, God reaches down to fallen man.

The purpose of the Law

The Law was never given as a means to obtain eternal life; it was given to show mankind the impossibility of obtaining righteousness by his own effort.

---

2 J.F. Strombeck, *Grace And Truth* (Strombeck Foundation, Moline, Ill. 1956 Edition), 11.

"Now we know that whatever the Law says, it speaks to those who are under the Law, that every mouth may be closed, and all the world may become accountable to God; because by the works of the Law no flesh will be justified in His sight; for through the Law comes the knowledge of sin." (Rom 3:19-20)

"And the Law came in that the transgression might increase; but where sin increased, grace abounded all the more." (Rom 5:20)

"The sting of death is sin, and the power of sin is the law..." (1 Cor 15:56)

"Why the Law then? It was added because of transgressions, having been ordained through angels by the agency of a mediator, until the seed should come to whom the promise had been made." (Gal 3:19)

"...we were kept in custody under the law... Therefore the Law has become our tutor to lead us to Christ..." (Gal 3:23-24)

The inability of the Law to justify

"...through Him forgiveness of sins is proclaimed to you, and through Him everyone who believes is freed from all things, from which you could not be freed through the Law of Moses." (Acts 13:38-39)

"...because by the works of the Law no flesh will be justified in His sight...." (Rom 3:20)

"For we maintain that a man is justified by faith apart from works of the Law." (Rom 3:28)

"For what the Law could not do, weak as it was through the flesh, God did: sending His own Son in the likeness of sinful flesh and as an offering for sin, He condemned sin in the flesh..." (Rom 8:3)

"For Christ is the end of the law for righteousness to everyone who believes." (Rom 10:4)

"Nevertheless knowing that a man is not justified by the works of the Law but through faith in Christ Jesus, even we have believed in Christ Jesus, that we may be justified by faith in Christ, and not by the works of the Law; since by the works of the Law shall no flesh be justified." (Gal 2:16)

"I do not nullify the grace of God; for if righteousness comes through the Law, then Christ died needlessly." (Gal 2:21)

"Therefore the Law has become our tutor to lead us to Christ, that we may be justified by faith." (Gal 3:24)

We see from the above that the Law was never intended to justify but was given to show us our need for a different kind of righteousness—the righteousness of God that is received by faith. Strombeck writes,

> Under law...condemnation is because man does not do all that the law demands and does do that which it forbids. In this the merit or demerit of man is the all important and deciding factor. The new condition for condemnation is not at all demerit on the part of man. It is in no way related to what man does. It is because of the failure of man to believe in, or to depend upon the merit of the Son of God.[3]

---

3 Strombeck, *Grace And Truth*, 46.

Because we are justified by faith apart from the works of the Law, Paul tells us in Romans 3:31 that we establish the Law through faith. That is, the Law's penalty is completely satisfied by Christ's death and the Law's purpose of bringing us to Christ is established. Because of the cross, man is not condemned because the Law is broken but because he has rejected Christ and in doing so has rejected the grace and provision for the Law's demands that came through Him.

SANCTIFICATION: CHRISTIAN LIFE BY GRACE, NOT LAW

The sad condition of most Christians is that they believe in Jesus Christ for eternal life but then try to put themselves back under Law to live the Christian life. There is something in us that leads us to try and depend on our own efforts to please God. Paul wrote the book of Galatians to deal with this very issue that we often call legalism. Webster defines legalism as, "strict, literal, or excessive conformity to the law or to a religious or moral code."[4] Legalism can affect both justification and sanctification. Merrill Tenney writes,

> Two general problems appear in Galatians: the problem of
> a salvation of the soul by works versus a salvation by faith
> and the problem of a perfection by works rather than a
> perfection by faith. The former is peculiarly the problem
> of the unsaved formalist whose religion consists chiefly in
> a negative attitude toward life expressed by prohibitions.
> Parallel to this problem and a logical counterpart to it is
> the problem of the believer who desires to be perfected
> in his moral and spiritual nature, and who relies upon
> the law for that perfection... Both of these problems may
> be subsumed under the one head of legalism for they
> are essentially the one question related to two spheres of

---

4 Merriam-Webster, I. 1996, c1993. *Merriam-Webster's collegiate dictionary.* Includes index. (10th ed.). Merriam-Webster: Springfield, Mass., U.S.A.

life… Galatians is directed against both of these errors, though in its exposition the second has generally received less attention.[5]

This very error made by the believers at Galatia of trying to live the Christian life by Law infuriated Paul. His words are very straight forward:

"You foolish Galatians, who has bewitched you… did you receive the Spirit by the works of the Law, or by hearing with faith? Are you so foolish? Having begun by the Spirit, are you now being perfected by the flesh?" (Gal 3:1-3)

In contrast to living the Christian life by the Law, Paul instructs us to walk by the Spirit:

"But I say walk by the Spirit and you will not carry out the desire of the flesh… If we live by the Spirit, let us also walk by the Spirit." (Gal 5:16, 25)

Strombeck notes, "To say that the moral standards of the law are an obligation upon believers is to insist upon a purely human standard of life for those who by regeneration have become a part of the new creation in Christ Jesus."[6] Grace through faith has always been God's method of saving man both eternally and temporally. Paul in Romans 14:23 says, *"…whatever is not from faith is sin."* Legalists fail to realize that their rules and regulations, which they depend upon themselves to fulfill, are not of faith and are therefore sinful. Strombeck makes this observation:

"They (legalists) accept certain acts as being sinful and subject to condemnation and are perfectly willing to condemn those that trespass those standards. They fail

---

5 Merrill C. Tenney, *Galatians: The Charter of Christian Liberty*, Wm. B. Eerdmans Pub. Co., Grand Rapids, MI, 1950. 27, 29.

6 Strombeck, *Grace And Truth*, 105.

utterly, however, to recognize what sin really is. No one who understands God's definition of sin: 'Whatsoever is not of faith is sin' (Rom. 14:23), can possibly be a legalist. The legalist little realizes that by his own legalism he is believing in himself instead of Him who God sent to be the object of faith. In whatever measure God's message is rejected, in that same measure is He rejected through Whom came grace and truth."[7]

While it is very tempting to use Law to try and get believers to behave, it never works! God's method is grace! Ron Merryman, writer and president of Merryman Ministires, outlines legalism as follows:

1. Legalism is the desire to "help" God improve upon our righteousness or to give Him more adequate reason to see us as righteous (than our simple faith in Christ's work). Galatians 2 illustrates the foolishness of this: Peter knew that justification, i.e., righteousness before God, was by simple faith in the work of Christ, yet he yielded to the legalists, so Paul had to reaffirm the truths of justification (Gal 2:11-21).

2. Legalism is human effort to approbate God. It seeks merit from God on the basis of human good.

3. Legalism usually expresses itself in a code or system of taboos. Legalistic people try to force their system of "dos" and "don'ts" on others.

4. Legalism is the opposite of grace.
   a. In the case of the believer, legalist codes are efforts to improve upon the work of Christ or upon what He provides in "Phase 2" of salvation.
   b. In the case of the unbeliever, legalistic codes seek God's approval apart from the work of Christ.

---

7 Strombeck, Grace And Truth, 72.

5. Legalism often results from a confusion in the mind of the new believer over the means of spirituality. In many churches, a system of works-spirituality is taught as in the following examples:

    a. "Follow a system of 'dos' and 'don'ts' and you will be spiritual" (each church or geographical area will have its own list);

    b. "Mimic the talk, mannerism, or dress of the super-spiritual ones";

    c. "Crucify yourself and you will be spiritual" (self-canceling out self—an impossibility!);

    d. Self-sacrifice or ascetic practices – "one is a super if he practices extreme self-denial" (The Hindus, Moslems and Roman Catholic hierarchy believe it, too.);

    e. Witnessing is often used as a basis of works-spirituality: "If you witness to x number of people each day, you will turn out a super-spiritual."

6. Legalism can only be properly understood by understanding the Pauline doctrines of grace, justification, spirituality by grace, and the resources of grace provision.

The legalist consistently confuses the means of spirituality with the results of true spirituality. A person who is spiritual will have a value system: He will not be a loose person; he will have some "dos" and "don'ts" in his life; he will find himself volitionally and spontaneously witnessing for Christ. But, he will not be doing or practicing these things in order to approbate God (Jesus and Jesus alone completed this approbation at Calvary); nor will he be doing these things in order to be spiritual; but he does them because he IS spiritual; meaning, he is in right relationship to the Holy Spirit, who alone provides the power and vitality to live the Christian life.[8]

---

8 Ronald C. Merryman, *Galatians: God's Antidote to Legalism* (Merryman Ministries, 5531 Spoked Wheel Drive, Colorado Springs, Colorado 80918, 1999), 36.

Clearly, legalism will ruin your Christian life. But doesn't grace open the door for licentious living? The opposite is actually true. As we have seen, grace teaches us to *live sensibly, righteously, and godly in this present age.* In the next chapter, we will take a look at our liberty in Christ and how we properly balance law and liberty.

Who gave Himself for us that He might redeem us
from every lawless deed...

CHAPTER 13:

GRACE AND LIBERTY

There are two errors that arise from misunderstanding grace. The first is what is called *antinomianism* which comes from the Greek words for 'without law.' Antinomianism basically teaches that once a person is justified in Christ, then all law is annulled, and that person can live as he or she pleases without regard to God's commands. The other error is legalism, teaching that we are saved by grace, but we are under obligation to keep the law (usually the moral code) to be accepted by God. The truth is, neither of these positions is biblical.

Ron Merryman summarizes these two errors well:

> ...Christianity is not legalism, nor is it antinomian. Legalism is a formal arrangement of the external matters of one's life in order to appear righteous... Legalism is a fleshly attitude that seeks to regulate behavior by conformity to a code. It then equates spirituality with the degree of that

conformity. Legalism concerns itself with externals and appearances. Legalism is not the existence of a rule, the observance of a principle or command, or a refraining from certain activities. The issue is the motivation that prompts the obedience: pride, self-glorification, false humility, and approbation-lust will make one an eminent legalist.... Christianity is not antinomian. ("against law"); it simply clarifies the purposes of the Law. It does embody some dos and don'ts. It most certainly has principles. The point is that these principles or commands or strictures are not fulfilled by human effort. Indeed, they are fulfilled totally through the indwelling Spirit of Christ and/or the grace provision of God. As a result, human merit and boasting are totally excluded. Gospel works are motivated by love and faith.[1]

So, what is the proper understanding of our freedom in Christ? Paul tells us in Galatians 5:1, *"It was for freedom that Christ set us free; therefore keep standing firm and do not be subject again to a yoke of slavery."* If we are totally free in Christ, does this mean that sin is not important? Jim Kirkwood writes,

That God's Grace brings the believer into the sphere of Total Freedom is the consistent testimony of the Pauline Epistles (Gal 5:1). That Christians have traditionally shrunk from this great Scriptural Truth is the record of history... Grace is Grace and Law is Law and a broken law demands a penalty, but how does one break Grace? It is unmerited favor, undeserved kindness. Law prescribes limits; Grace is limitless... Grace says 'Stop your doing...lay your deadly doing down and trust.' Trust in what your Substitute has

---

1 Ron Merryman, *The Believer & The Mosaic Law* (Merryman Ministries, Colorado Springs, Colorado, 2000), 18-19.

already done… The objection will always be raised that this much freedom…total freedom from all condemnation… will be an open invitation to sin. This type of thinking overlooks several things. First of all, that Christ teaches the superior motivation of Grace. Grace is not an incitement to sin, but an inducement to holiness… Second, it is Law and not Grace that incites man's sinful nature and prompts more sin. Law is a system of conditional blessing and cursing… Grace brings with it a new nature that cannot sin, that can only respond positively to the indwelling Spirit of God.[2]

Musician and Bible student John Fischer wrote a musical called *The New Covenant* in 1975 which included these insightful words:

"Do this and live," the law commands,
But gives me neither feet nor hands.
A better way His grace doth bring,
It bids me fly and gives me wings.[3]

Freedom from Law is not license to sin. It is freedom from a works-based system that appeals to our human flesh that we cannot possibly fulfill. What about the commands of the New Testament? Does our freedom in Christ remove us from any obligations to the commands in Scripture? Certainly not! Desiring to obey the commands of God in the Scripture does not make us legalists if we are doing so by the power of the Spirit with the proper motivation. Even though, in our freedom, all things are lawful for us, Paul does put some restrictions on our liberty,

"All things are lawful for me, but all things are not profitable.
All things are lawful for me, but I will not be mastered by

---

2 Jim Kirkwood, *God's Grace: License or Liberty?* Web Article http://www.gracebeliever. com/articles/articles/licenseorliberty.htm.
3 John Fisher, *Alleluia*, The New Covenant © 1975 by Lexicon Music, Inc.

anything." (1 Cor 6:12)

"But take care lest this liberty of yours somehow become a stumbling block to the weak." (1 Cor 8:9)

"All things are lawful, but not all things are profitable. All things are lawful, but not all things edify. (1 Cor 10:23)

When Paul refers to "all things," he, unlike the Corinthians who coined the slogan, means all things not specifically forbidden in Scripture. This is crystal clear in the immediate (6:1-20) and broader context (8:1-11:1). Paul is referring to our liberty in unspecified areas. There is much freedom in our walk with Christ. We can choose any car, any apartment or house, any clothes, any food, any sport, etc., yet with two prominent restrictions.

The first restriction on our liberty is how our actions affect other believers. Using our freedom or liberty for selfish purposes without regard to our brother or sister in Christ is wrong. In 1 Corinthians 10:23-33, Paul instructs us to put the welfare of others above our own and to do everything for God's glory,

"Let no one seek his own good, but that of his neighbor." (v. 24)

"Whether, then, you eat or drink or whatever you do, do all to the glory of God." (v. 31)

In 1 Corinthians 8:12, he is clear that we sin against Christ when we cause our brother to stumble.

The second restriction concerns addictions. We should not be *mastered by anything.* To be addicted to anything, even those things not forbidden in Scripture, is wrong. Most things in life like hunting, sports, television, work, the internet, etc., are morally neutral. However, when anything becomes an addiction, something we either can't stop or something that is keeping us from doing what we know is more important, then it is wrong.

The bottom line is that our liberty in Christ should be controlled by our love for Him. License asks the question, "What can I get away with?" or uses the rationalization, "I'm not under law so I can do whatever I please and if you challenge me, you are a legalist." Liberty rejoices in our freedom in Christ and always looks to how we can please Him. Liberty frees us from rules and regulations and teaches us to trust the indwelling Spirit for our strength and power. Grace teaches freedom. Grace teaches liberty. Grace teaches love and devotion to Christ. Grace is not an incitement to sin, but an inducement to holiness!

Who gave Himself for us to redeem us from every lawless deed…

CHAPTER 14:
WHOM THE LORD LOVES HE DISCIPLINES

How does the Lord *redeem us from every lawless deed*? He loves us as his children and as a loving father disciplines his children, so also the Lord disciplines us. Discipline in Scripture can be viewed from two perspectives. Both are based in God's love for us as His children. We are disciplined as sons when we have unconfessed sin in our lives, and we are also disciplined as sons for the purpose of becoming more Christlike.

It is important to note that discipline as sons has nothing to do with condemnation or eternal judgment for sin. Jesus said, *"Truly, truly, I say to you, he who hears My word, and believes Him who sent Me has eternal life, and does not come into judgment, but has passed out of death into life"* (Jn 5:24). Chafer writes, "One who stands in the imputed merit of Christ, as every saved person does, could not come into condemnation;

nevertheless, for sin in which a Christian willfully persists there may be chastisement from the Father, who is Himself a perfect disciplinarian."[1] The very moment we believe, we receive a righteousness from God that is imputed to us. However, we still have a sin nature and the possibility for sin in our lives as believers is ever present. 1 John makes it clear that fellowship with the Father depends on our walking in the light and also, when we realize there is sin in our lives, our immediate confession.

DISCIPLINE OR CHASTISEMENT FOR UNCONFESSED SIN

Discussing sin in the life of the believer, Jody Dillow makes the following statement:

> Once a man is born again in Christ, he is now in God's family, and as any human father would, our divine Father takes a more personal interest in the moral behavior of those who belong to Him than to those who are outside the household of faith. The Scriptures set forth three consequences of sin: discipline, death, and disinheritance... The principle is that discipline results in judgment in time or forfeiture in eternity but not loss of salvation.[2]

Discipline

> *"But if we judged ourselves rightly, we should not be judged. But when we are judged, we are disciplined by the Lord in order that we may not be condemned along with the world."* (1 Cor 11:31-32)

One of the purposes of discipline is to bring believers to the place of repentance and confession so that their fellowship and walk with God will be restored. The believer who does not confess and refuses

---

1 Lewis Sperry Chafer, *Systematic Theology (Vol. VII*, Dallas Seminary Press, 1948), 71.

2 Joseph C. Dillow, *The Reign of the Servant Kings* (Schoettle Publishing Co, Miami Springs, Florida, 1992), 341.

to learn from God's discipline is storing up judgment at the Judgment Seat of Christ (Bema Seat). Both the Bema Seat (where believers will be judged), and the Great White Throne (where non-believers will be judged), are judgments of works or deeds. Therefore, the believer who lives a carnal life with unconfessed sin is in danger of receiving the same condemnation for his works as the unbeliever will receive. Chafer writes,

> It is the grace of God which waits thus for the believer to act first in his own behalf respecting his sin. However, if the sinning child of God will not thus judge himself by a full confession, it becomes necessary for the Father, being the perfect disciplinarian that He is, to bring His child into judgment. This is the force of the Apostle's words: 'If we would judge ourselves, we should not be judged.' The voluntary act of self-judgment satisfies every divine demand and no judgment from the Father will be imposed. It is only when the Christian withholds his confession and by so much assumes the attitude of self-justification concerning his sin, or through love of it refuses to be adjusted to the holy will of God, that the Father must bring him into the place of correction…. The issue is not one of sustaining a union with the Father…it is rather the issue of respecting communion or fellowship.[3]

Death

> *"But let a man examine himself, and so let him eat of the bread and drink of the cup. For he who eats and drinks, eats and drinks judgment to himself, if he does not judge the body rightly. For this reason many among you are weak and sick, and a number sleep."* (1 Cor 11:28-30)

---

3 Lewis Sperry Chafer, *Systematic Theology, Vol. VI,* (Dallas Seminary Press, 1948), 240-241.

Paul's warning, in the context of believers participating in the Lord's supper with unconfessed sin in their lives, is clear: sickness and even physical death are possible. There are a number of passages in Scripture that indicate God may take home the believer who fails to respond to discipline. Note the words of James in James 5:19-20,

> *"My brethren, if any among you strays from the truth, and one turns him back, let him know that he who turns a sinner from the error of his way will save his soul from death, and will cover a multitude of sins."*

James is clearly talking to believers and gives a sober warning that physical death may be the consequence of persistent error and sin. John writes these sobering words in 1 John 5:16-17,

> *"If anyone sees his brother committing a sin not leading to death, he shall ask and God will for him give life to those who commit sin not leading to death. There is a sin leading to death; I do not say that he should make request for this. All unrighteousness is sin, and there is a sin not leading to death."*

Since a brother already has eternal life, the life here must be physical life and the death physical death. The point is that, we as believers can come to the place in our lives because of persistent sin, that God chooses to take us home to Himself. God, in his mercy and grace, is very longsuffering with his children and we can never humanly say, "God is going to do this or that to a person." However, it is a very dangerous thing to continue in willful sin as believers and put ourselves in the position of severe discipline from God. In 1 Corinthians 5:5, Paul turned the brother who persisted in immorality over to Satan for the destruction of his flesh *"...that his spirit may be saved in the day of the Lord Jesus."*

Perhaps the most obvious case of this divine discipline occurs in Acts 5 when Ananias and Sapphira lie to the Holy Spirit and God strikes them dead publicly. God is serious about sin in the life of His children, and it appears that those sins, having to do with pride and arrogance which characterize willful sin, are most severely judged. If we compare Numbers 15:30-31 with Hebrews 10:26-27, we see that willful sin must be judged because it is a denial of Christ's provision for our daily walk. 1 John 1:7 tells us that the blood of Christ cleanses from all sin when we confess and walk in fellowship. To willfully sin is to deny the provision and sacrifice God provided for our walk with him. This is why the writer of Hebrews says:

> *"For if we go on sinning willfully after receiving the knowledge of the truth, there no longer remains a sacrifice for sins, but a certain terrifying expectation of judgment, and the fury of a fire which will consume the adversaries."* (Heb 10:26-27)

Loss of inheritance

Dillow says, "The final consequence of protracted carnality is forfeiture of reward and stinging rebuke when the King returns to establish His rule. No tragedy could be greater than for the Christian, saved by grace and given unlimited possibilities, to forfeit all of this and fail to participate in the future reign of the servant kings."[4] Many passages of Scripture that are often misinterpreted to teach loss of eternal life in reality are teaching the loss of inheritance in the millennial kingdom because of sin in the believer's life. For further detailed study on this subject, see Joseph Dillow's book *The Reign of the Servant Kings*.

DISCIPLINE FOR THE PURPOSE OF HOLINESS

Discipline often has a greater purpose than just correction for sin. The key passage is Hebrews 12:1-11. It should be noted that the motive for *divine discipline* is *divine love*! Notice God's instructions to us:

- View discipline correctly (v. 5)
- Discipline is based in God's love (v. 6)

---

4 Dillow, *The Reign of the Servant Kings*, 344.

- Every son (every believer) is a partaker of discipline (vv. 6-8)
- We should respect God for His discipline in our lives (v. 9)
- God's discipline is always for our good (v. 10)
- God's purpose for discipline is that we might share His holiness (v. 10)
- The process of discipline is not a joyous one, but often a sorrowful process (v. 11)
- The result of the process for those who are trained is the peaceful fruit of righteousness (v. 11)

Verses 1 through 4 of Hebrews 12 help us maintain the proper attitude through discipline. Our strength for the race of life we run comes from our focus on the Lord Jesus who ran the perfect race! Hebrews 12:6 speaks of discipline and scourging. Some have said that discipline is an ongoing process, but that scourging is not often repeated. Scourging has been likened to those intense instances when God has to break the rebellious human will. Once this occurs in the life of a son, it usually doesn't have to be repeated. Whatever the meaning, it is clear that scourging is much more severe than discipline.

We must remember that not all suffering is a result of sin or discipline for sin. Christ suffered because of His righteousness and because of the evil of man. Paul prayed, *"that I may know Him, and the power of His resurrection and the fellowship of His sufferings, being conformed to His death"* (Phil 3:10). Job also suffered because God allowed Satan, to a point, to cause him harm. We must be careful not to immediately assume that when someone is suffering or when some calamity comes upon them that it is because of unconfessed sin in their life. Also, at times God will use discipline *because of sin* in our lives to also teach us and help us become more Christ like. In other words, He will take our failure and use it to teach us more about godliness. James encourages in James 1:2-4, *"Consider it all joy, my brethren, when you encounter various trials, knowing that the testing of your faith produces endurance. And let endurance have its perfect result, so that you may be perfect and complete, lacking in nothing."*

Ultimately, all discipline is based on our family relationship. Because God is our Father and we are his children, He is intimately concerned with us. He is very pro-active in His relationship with us and uses every means of discipline to help bring us into conformity with His Son. If we resist His discipline, the consequences can be severe, even to the loss of physical life. More tragic than physical loss is the potential loss of reward and inheritance in the kingdom.

And to purify for Himself a people for His own possession...

CHAPTER 15:
THE BELIEVER'S SECURITY

What a comforting thought that God sees us as *a people for His own possession*! There is great security in our relationship with God. Indeed, eternal security is the foundation for effective Christian living. However, a number of pertinent questions have been raised concerning the believer's security. Questions such as: Is the believer saved forever? Does eternal security promote sin in the believer's life? What if a believer decides to stop believing? What about a believer who continually sins? Do good works in someone's life mean that person is saved and secure? Does the lack of good works in someone's life mean that person is not saved and secure? Is it possible to know you are saved? Is it possible to be saved and not know you are secure? Must we **C**ommit, **O**bey, and **P**ersevere to be sure we have eternal life?

Properly understanding eternal security gives true freedom (not fear) for living the Christian life. To believe in Christ is to enter into covenant relationship with God Himself. There are many Divine Eternal

Effects (results) that occur the moment someone believes in Jesus Christ. These results are based entirely on the character of the Trinity working on behalf of the believer and can never be changed, or else the character of God Himself is at stake. To admit that there is nothing one can do to *receive* eternal life, but to say there is something the believer can do, or not do, to *lose* eternal life, is to elevate man's behavior and power beyond that of God. To deny the doctrine of eternal security is to not understand clearly the issue of sin. To deny the doctrine of eternal security is to not understand clearly the Savior. What must be answered biblically are as follows:

1. Who is this Person who died on a cross?
2. Why did He die?
3. What did He accomplish when He died?

We have previously seen that Jesus was God in the flesh and therefore the only person in all the universe who was qualified to pay the debt required for mankind's sin. We have also seen that the finished work of Christ included redemption, reconciliation, and propitiation. In other words, the sin debt was paid IN FULL by Jesus on the cross. Regeneration, justification, and the receipt of imputed righteousness occur the moment someone believes in Jesus. To say that believers could lose their salvation would mean that they would have to be unborn spiritually and God would have to take away the righteousness that He already had put to their account. These concepts are totally foreign to the clear teachings of Scripture.

SOME SCRIPTURAL ARGUMENTS FOR ETERNAL SECURITY

The nature of the life that is given.

The word eternal, αἰώνιος, *aionios,* is an adjective that describes the word life, ζωή, *zoe.* In other words, when we believe in Christ, we receive a certain kind of life, *eternal* life. The Greek lexicons give the meanings "without end, never to cease, everlasting" for this adjective. The obvious question is: How can something cease whose very definition is "never ceasing"? A related thought is that God could have used any adjective He wished to convey what we receive at the moment of belief. It could have been *victorious life* or *holy life* or *probationary life* or *abundant life* or many other descriptive terms. The word He used was **eternal**!

> *"For God so loved the world, that He gave His only begotten Son, that whoever believes in Him should not perish, but have eternal life."* (Jn 3:16)

Eternal life is a present possession.

The Bible does not teach that eternal life is awarded when a person dies (if he has been good enough or persevered to the end) but that it is a gift received the moment of belief. Notice these couple of verses: John 5:24, *"Truly, truly, I say to you, he who hears My word, and believes Him who sent Me, **has** eternal life, and **does not come** into judgment, but **has passed** out of death into life"*, and John 6:47, *"Truly, truly, I say to you, he who believes **has** eternal life."*

Part of eternal life is the present possession of knowledge of God. Notice Jesus' words in John 17:3, *"And this is eternal life, that they may know Thee, the only true God, and Jesus Christ whom Thou hast sent."*

Eternal life is a gift.

> *"For by grace you have been saved through faith; and that not of yourselves, it is the Gift of God; not as a result of works, that no one should boast."* (Eph 2:8-9)

If salvation (eternal life) is truly a gift, then it could never be lost unless God were to take back His gift. However, we know that God is immutable, unchanging in His nature, and His gifts and calling cannot be undone. Paul says it this way in Romans 11:29, *"...for the gifts and the calling of God are irrevocable."*

Eternal life is received by faith and not by works.

Because eternal life is received by faith and not by works, works cannot possibly have a part in obtaining or keeping eternal life. As a matter of fact, grace and works are said to be mutually exclusive of each other.

> *"But if it is by grace, it is no longer on the basis of works, otherwise grace is no longer grace."* (Rom 11:6)

How can something that is a gift and received by faith apart from works then all of a sudden be kept by works? Paul says if very clearly in Romans 4:4-6,

> *"Now to the one who works, his wage is not reckoned as a favor, but as what is due. But to the one who does not work, but believes in Him who justifies the ungodly, his faith is reckoned as righteousness, just as David also speaks of the blessing upon the man to whom God reckons righteousness apart from works."*

Our eternal security is dependent on the strength of God and not our efforts.

> Jesus said, *"My sheep hear My voice, and I know them, and they follow Me; and I give eternal life to them, and they shall never perish; and no one shall snatch them out of My hand. My Father, who has given them to Me, is greater than all; and no one is able to snatch them out of the Father's hand. I and the Father are one".* (Jn 10:27-30)

It is the strength of God the Son and the Father which guarantees this condition of safety. Sometimes, we hear such ideas as, "No one can snatch us out of God's hand but we can jump out if we decide to stop believing." For someone to remove himself from the security of the Father's hand would be to elevate himself above God. When my children were small, I would often hold their hands as we crossed streets or did other activities where they needed my protection. I would never let someone come along and grab them away from me, but I also would never let them pull themselves away in those situations. As their father, I held them securely whether or not they wanted to be held! God does the same for His children. Once I become His child by faith (John 1:12), I am held securely by His power, not mine!

Our eternal security is dependent on His faithfulness, not ours.

> *"It is a trustworthy statement: For if we died with Him, we shall also live with Him;*
> *If we endure, we shall also reign with Him; If we deny Him, He also will deny us;*
> *If we are faithless, He remains faithful; for He cannot deny Himself." (2 Tim 2:11-13)*

Notice the four stanzas of this statement. The first states the certainty of our salvation. Our belief in Christ causes the old man to be crucified and the new man to be born from above. The second and third stanzas are a parallel. Endurance (faithful service in the context of hardship and suffering) results in reward and reign with Christ. Denial, not being faithful as a believer, causes Christ to deny us reward and reign. However, in the fourth stanza, if we are faithless, He remains faithful based on His very character as God. To cast us out of the family of God because we stop believing would be to deny Christ's very person as the eternal 'mercy seat' who made the once-for-all sacrifice.

We are secure because we are objects of God's love.
Every person is either the object of God's wrath (Eph 2:3, Jn 3:36) or the object of God's love (Jn 13:1, Jn 17:23, Eph 2:4, 1 Jn 3:1). That relationship to God is determined on whether or not we have

believed in Jesus Christ. As a believer, notice the security we have in the love of God:

> *"For I am convinced that neither death, nor life, nor angels, nor principalities, nor things present, nor things to come, nor powers, nor height, nor depth, nor any other created thing, shall be able to separate us from the love of God which is in Christ Jesus our Lord."* (Rom 8:38-39)

J.F. Strombeck, in his book *Shall Never Perish* first written in 1936, makes these statements about the love of God:

> If it be possible for one who has been saved to be lost, it must of necessity be possible for one who has been the object of the love of God to be taken out of that position and made the object of the wrath of God. Does any Scripture passage teach that? Definitely, No. On the contrary, it is taught that God loves His own with and everlasting love (Jer. 31:3)....
> It is, therefore, a flat denial of God's Word to say that a man can separate himself from God's love. If anything is emphatically taught in the Bible, it is that when man has become the object of the everlasting love of God, there is no change in that condition.[1]

We are secure because our glorification is already accomplished.
Notice the unbroken chain:

> *"For whom He foreknew, He also predestined to be conformed to the image of His Son, that He might be the first-born among many brethren; and whom He predestined, these He also called; and whom He called, these He also justified; and whom He justified, these He also glorified."* (Rom 8:29-30)

---

1 Strombeck, J.F. *Shall Never Perish* (Dunham Publishers, Findlay, Ohio, Ninth Edition 1964), 75-76.

All of these events are things that God has done for the saved one. All are in the past tense, therefore, already accomplished! Again, Strombeck summarizes well,

> ...believers are already glorified and that it is but the manifestation of the reality that is still in the future. There are things which God has already accomplished, but the manifestation thereof has been delayed until later. Thus, Christ is said to be the 'Lamb foreordained before the foundation of the world, but manifest in these last times' (1 Pet. 1:20). Similarly, the believer is already glorified. 'Whom He justified, them He also glorified.' But the manifestation thereof is in the future. 'Your life is hid with Christ in God. When Christ, Who is our life, shall appear, then shall we also appear with Him in glory' (Col.3:3, 4). *The glorification has taken place, though appearance in glory is in the future and in the meantime the believer's life is 'hid with Christ in God.' Can anyone be more secure?* If one who is saved can be lost, it must have to be by taking such an one from his place in glory where he is *hid in God.* Certainly no one dares to say that this is possible."[2]

Our security in Christ is also insured by the work of the Holy Spirit. The purpose of the Holy Spirit's presence in the life of the believer is an assurance of eternal security. One of the truths of regeneration is that it is by the Holy Spirit. Jesus makes this clear in John 3:3-6,

> *"Jesus answered and said to him, 'Truly, truly, I say to you, unless one is born again, he cannot see the kingdom of God.' Nicodemus said to Him, 'How can a man be born*

---

2 Strombeck, *Shall Never Perish*, 60-61.

when he is old? He cannot enter a second time into his mother's womb and be born, can he?' Jesus answered, 'Truly, truly, I say to you, unless one is born of water and the Spirit, he cannot enter into the kingdom of God. That which is born of the flesh is flesh, and that which is born of the Spirit is spirit.'"

In Titus 3:4-5, Paul states,

"But when the kindness of God our Savior and His love for mankind appeared, He saved us, not on the basis of deeds which we have done in righteousness, but according to His mercy, by the washing of regeneration and renewing by the Holy Spirit..."

Peter tells us that this new birth, because it is based on God's Word, is imperishable!

"...for you have been born again not of seed which is perishable but imperishable, that is, through the living and abiding word of God." (1 Pet 1:23)

There are three particular aspects of the Holy Spirit's work that we will consider in relation to eternal security.

THE INDWELLING OF THE SPIRIT

In John 14, Jesus promises the disciples that He is going to prepare dwelling places for them in heaven and assures them that He will come again. In this context of His departure, Jesus promises that the Father will send the Holy Spirit as a Helper and Comforter *forever*! However, the Spirit's relationship to all believers after the day of Pentecost (Acts 2) would be radically different from all believers up until that time. Until the day of Pentecost, the Spirit abided with believers. From that moment on, the Spirit indwells all believers!

"And I will ask the Father, and He will give you another Helper, that He may be with you forever, that is the Spirit of truth, whom the world cannot receive, because it does not behold Him or know Him, but you know Him because He abides with you, and will be in you." (Jn 14:16-17)

For a believer to lose their salvation would mean that the indwelling Holy Spirit would have to leave or 'un-indwell' the person. This is directly opposed to the teaching of Jesus that the Spirit would indwell *forever*. It is true that the Holy Spirit can be grieved (Eph 4:30) and quenched (1 Thess 5:19) by sin and disobedience in the life of the believer, but He is never said to be taken away. Paul makes it very clear that only God's children have the Holy Spirit:

"But if anyone does not have the Spirit of Christ, he does not belong to Him." (Rom 8:9b)

THE BAPTISM OF THE SPIRIT

Chafer writes,

The Greek word - βαπτίζω (baptizo) literally means to immerse or submerge. A secondary meaning which is always used when referring to the Spirit's baptism in the New Testament refers to the influence which one thing may have over another. Since the Holy Spirit is received by every believer at the moment he is saved, he is thus baptized by the Spirit, having been brought under the influence of the Spirit... Because of this great achievement on the part of the Spirit, the believer is from that moment in Christ and is thus brought under the influence of His Headship.[3]

---

3 Chafer, Vol. VI, 33.

Strong's Concordance offers additional insight into this word,

> to overwhelm. *Additional Information:* Not to be confused with 911, bapto. The clearest example that shows the meaning of baptizo is a text from the Greek poet and physician Nicander, who lived about 200 B.C. It is a recipe for making pickles and is helpful because it uses both words. Nicander says that in order to make a pickle, the vegetable should first be 'dipped' (bapto) into boiling water and then 'baptised' (baptizo) in the vinegar solution. Both verbs concern the immersing of vegetables in a solution. But the first is temporary. The second, the act of baptising the vegetable, produces a permanent change. When used in the New Testament, this word more often refers to our union and identification with Christ than to our water baptism.[4]

Paul tells us in Ephesians 4:5 that there is *"...one Lord, one faith, one baptism..."* It is this baptism of the Spirit that places every believer, at the moment of belief, into the Body of Christ, as stated in 1 Corinthians 12:13, *"For by one Spirit we were all baptized into one body..."* Our union with Christ is always seen as permanent in the New Testament.

THE SEALING OF THE SPIRIT

Sealed as to Position

Every instance of a seal in Scripture *"...denotes an unalterable position of those who are sealed."*[5] In Revelation 7:2-8, the 144,000 servants of God who are sealed on their foreheads are protected by God from

---

4 Strong, J. 1996. *The exhaustive concordance of the Bible : Showing every word of the test of the common English version of the canonical books, and every occurrence of each word in regular order.* (electronic ed.). Woodside Bible Fellowship.: Ontario.

5 Strombeck, *Shall Never Perish*, 72.

harm. When Daniel is thrown into the lion's den, the stone at the mouth of the den is sealed with the king's signet ring "...*so that nothing might be changed in regard to Daniel* (Dan 6:17)." In Revelation 20:2-3, Satan is thrown into the abyss and God shuts and seals the abyss over him for 1,000 years.

In all these cases, the seal is permanent in relation to the related action. This is exactly what the Holy Spirit does for the believer in Ephesians 4:30:

> "*And do not grieve the Holy Spirit of God, by whom* **you were sealed** *for the day of redemption.*"

Sealed as to ownership

> "*In Him, you also, after listening to the message of truth, the gospel of your salvation, having also believed,* **you were sealed in Him with the Holy Spirit of promise,** *who is given as a pledge of our inheritance, with a view to the redemption* **of God's own possession,** *to the praise of His glory.*" (Eph 1:13-14)

The seal of the Holy Spirit denotes ownership. Everyone who believes in Christ is purchased by His precious blood and becomes His very own. The seal of the Holy Spirit is the guarantee of this ownership and since it cannot be broken, believers are secure. It is always the one who seals who is responsible for the object upon which the seal is placed.

Sealed as an earnest of our inheritance

An earnest is a payment made by the purchaser to guarantee the completion of the transaction by him. In Ephesians 1:11, believers are said to have obtained an inheritance, and that inheritance is by the very will of God. As believers, we have not yet entered into possession of this inheritance, but verse 14 goes on to say that the Holy Spirit is our *earnest* or *pledge* of that inheritance. To say that a believer can be lost is to say that God will not or cannot honor His earnest payment.

The eternal security of the believer is a doctrine that is well grounded in Scripture. It is grounded in the finished work of Christ. God, as our heavenly father, may discipline us as His children, but He will never cast us out of His family!

Zealous for good deeds...

CHAPTER 16:

THE ROLE OF WORKS IN OUR SALVATION

A t times, those of us who believe in the free grace of God are criticized for promoting a lax moral lifestyle with no motivation to serve God through good works. John MacArthur is typical of this charge. He writes, "True faith is not lip service. Our Lord himself pronounced condemnation on those who worshipped him with their lips but not with their lives (Matt 15:7-9). He does not become anyone's Savior until a person receives him for who he is—Lord of all (Acts 10:36)."[1] In other words, if a professed believer hasn't made Jesus Lord of all and demonstrated that lordship with good works, then he or she is not a true believer. Alan P. Stanley, Reformed Australian Bible professor and writer, goes ever further when he writes, "...it is probably more accurate to speak of works as the condition for final

---

1 John F. MacArthur, Jr., *The Gospel According to Jesus* (Grand Rapids, Michigan, Zondervan), 35.

salvation into the eschatological kingdom… By condition we mean that if (post conversion) works (e.g., endurance, love, mercy, forgiveness) are not present then final salvation will not be granted."[2] Both of the above authors are promoting a works-based gospel. They are adding good works to the backside of faith as a proof or test of the genuineness of that faith. The problem with backloading the gospel with works as a proof of final salvation is that it takes away the security of the believer. It also has the tendency to promote legalism and fruit inspection. What does Free Grace theology actually teach about the role of works?

Free Grace theology promotes good works as the expected response in the life of a believer. Understanding the Judgment Seat of Christ puts the role of good works in a proper light. Indeed, the New Testament is full of commands to do good works. In Matthew 5:16, Jesus taught, *"Let your light shine before men in such a way that they may see your good works and glorify your Father who is in heaven."* Paul, in Ephesians 2:8, distinguishes between the gift of God and works, and then in verse 9 promotes good works saying, *"For by grace you have been saved through faith; and that not of yourselves, it is the gift of God; not as a result of works, so that no one may boast. For we are his workmanship, created in Christ Jesus for good works, which God prepared beforehand that we would walk in them."* Free Grace theology sees good works in the life of the believer as God's design, for we were created in Christ Jesus *for good works.* In Colossians 1:9-10, Paul writes, *"For this reason also, since the day we heard of it, we have not ceased to pray for you and to ask that you may be filled with the knowledge of His will in all spiritual wisdom and understanding, so that you will walk in a manner worthy of the Lord, to please Him in all respects, bearing fruit in every good work and increasing in the knowledge of God."* Notice that the more we are filled with the knowledge of His will, the more we will walk in a worthy manner, and we will bear fruit in good works. Indeed,

---

2 Alan P. Stanley, *Did Jesus Teach Salvation by Works? The Role of Works in Salvation in the Synoptic Gospels* (Eugene, OR, Pickwick Publications, 2006), 334.

good works should be the normal result of studying the Scripture and walking with the Lord. Paul writes in 2 Timothy 3:16-17, *"All Scripture is inspired by God and profitable for teaching, for reproof, for correction, for training in righteousness; so that the man of God may be adequate, equipped for every good work."* Good works are results of learning and being reproved by the Word of God. It is in that growth and knowledge of the Scriptures that good works may flourish.

What about the passages that seem to teach the necessity of works for salvation? I believe that in context, all the seemingly work-based passages can be explained with a grace viewpoint. For example, James 2:14-26 has been often quoted as promoting good works for proof of true conversion. This is where context is so important. The theme of James is faith working in the everyday life of believers. The theme of James is stated in 1:19, *"This you know my beloved brethren. But let everyone be quick to hear, slow to speak, and slow to anger."* We can outline the book based on this purpose statement as such: Quick to Hear (1:21-2:26); Slow to Speak (3:1-18); and Slow to Anger (4:1-5:6). Contextually, James is written to believers to encourage their growth and walk with the Lord.

James 2:14-29 is one of the most misunderstood passages in the Bible. Because of the *supposed* tension (disagreement) between Paul's statements in Romans 4 concerning justification by faith alone and James' statements about justification by faith and works, numerous interpretations have arisen.

Those who understand justification in this passage as referring to eternal justification (going to heaven) would say:

1. Faith and works are necessary for eternal life.
2. The right kind of faith (faith that produces works) is necessary for eternal life.
   a. The Arminian – If you do not continue in good works, then you risk losing your salvation.
   b. The Calvinist – If you do not persevere in good works, then you did not have the right kind of faith. In other words, you are not truly saved.

Those who understand justification in this passage as referring to temporal justification (justification before men) would say:

1.   Faith and works are necessary for *the believer* to be justified before men and at the Judgment Seat.
2.   There is only one kind of faith.

Several key issues emerge from the views above:

1.   What is the nature of faith?
2.   What does the word "saved" mean?
3.   Is there one or two "justifications" in view?
4.   What is the objector saying, and where does his quote end?

As we go verse by verse through this passage, we will address these issues.

VERSE 14

My brethren, if a man says – If we are honest with the context of James, then clearly believers are being addressed.

Can (that) faith save him? – The word *that* is an interpretive addition. The KJV and NKJV simply state, "Can faith save him?" The NIV states, "Can *such* faith save him?" The NASB states, "Can *that* faith save him?" The issue here is the nature of faith. Those who hold to Lordship salvation argue that there are two kinds of faith in the New Testament: *saving faith* and *non-saving* faith.

Yet careful analysis of the word faith (*pistos, pisteuo*) does not support this idea. Dave Anderson states, "...we have no conclusive evidence in the NT for different categories of faith. Different levels, yes; different categories, no. Faith is faith, real faith, genuine faith, through and through... Saving faith obviously needs to be tethered to the person and work of Jesus Christ."[3]

So why do some say there are two kinds of faith? This has been added to fit the Reformed and Lordship understanding of this passage.

3 Anderson, *Free Grace Soteriology*, 189.

The clear answer to James' question is that faith cannot *save* the man who has no works! This brings up the issue of what is meant by the word *save*. James uses the word *save* (*sozo*) five times in his epistle (1:21, 2:14, 4:12, 5:15, 5:20). In context, every use refers to temporal deliverance and not salvation from hell. James has just stated in 2:12-13 that we will be judged by the law of liberty at the Judgment Seat of Christ. Faith that has no works cannot *save* a person at that judgment.

VERSES 15-16   AN ILLUSTRATION

The poor brother or sister – If you do not put actions with your faith, it is useless for the one in need. A benediction cannot save a starving man from death; only bread can do that.

VERSE 17

James has no thought of whether or not this person is a believer and possesses eternal life. His wish is to admonish Christians to practice their faith by doing good works. The choice of the word "dead" is perfectly suited to the context. Just as idle words cannot save a brother from death in the absence of life's necessities, a dead (not working) faith cannot save us from the death-dealing consequences of sin. Therefore, faith not expressed is by itself, or ineffective.

VERSES 18-19   THE OBJECTOR

This literary method of using the mouth of an imaginary objector is used often in Scripture (Rom 9:19-20, 1 Cor 15:35-36). It is called a diatribe. The question is: Where does the objector start and where does he end his statements? The NIV and the NKJV translate only the first half of the verse in quotation marks. The NASB translates all of verse 18 in quotation marks. In the context of the argument, it seems best to take all of verse 18 and 19 as the words of the objector. Using the Greek word order, the objector's statement would be, *"You have faith and I have works. Show me your faith from your works, and I will show you, from my works, my faith. You believe that there is one God; you do well. The demons also believe, and tremble."*

The objector's argument is that there is not a close relation between faith and works. His illustration is that even demons believe but it does not produce the same result as a man's faith.

In other words, the objector is saying, "Don't criticize my faith because I don't do such and such a thing."

VERSE 20

You foolish fellow – This begins James' reply to the objector's argument. James is saying that the argument is senseless and that the objector is foolish to make it.

Faith without works is dead (useless) – James is not saying that without works as a proof, faith never existed. He is saying that it is dead in the sense of being useless.

VERSES 21-22   THE ILLUSTRATION OF ABRAHAM

Justified by works when he offered up Isaac – Abraham offered up Isaac in Genesis 22. Abraham is declared righteous in Genesis 15:6. There are at least 15 or 20 years between these two events. When God declares believers righteous, they never lose their righteous standing before Him. Abraham's subsequent justification refers to a second declaration of his righteousness, but this time, his works declared him righteous.

You see – This is singular, indicating that Abraham is still responding to the objector of verses 18-19.

Faith was perfected – Abraham's faith in the midst of trial was perfected, strengthened and matured, by his works. Note the confidence of Abraham's faith in Hebrews 11:17-19.

VERSE 23

The Scripture was fulfilled – When Abraham put his faith to work, the implications of his original faith were realized and Genesis 15:6 was fulfilled.

He was called the friend of God – When believers are justified by works, they achieve an intimacy with God that is manifest to others.

Abraham is recognized as the friend of God by three religions: Judaism, Islam, and Christianity. Heed the words of Jesus in John 15:14, *"You are my friends, if you do what I command you."*

VERSE 24

You see – Plural. Now James returns to the readers of his epistle.

A man is justified by works, and not by faith alone – There are two kinds of justifications. The word *alone* is an adverb and modifies the verb *justified*. The translation should read, *"You see then that a man is justified by works, and not only (justified) by faith."*

By faith justification = Before God.

By works justification = Before men.

VERSE 25   THE ILLUSTRATION OF RAHAB

In contrast to Abraham, the patriarch of Israel, James uses Rahab the prostitute to demonstrate justification by works. Note carefully Hebrews 11:31 and Joshua 2. Rahab was justified before God when she believed. She was not justified by her works until she received the spies and helped them escape to safety. As a result, she and her family were saved (delivered) when Israel defeated Jericho (Josh 6:25). Rahab became the great, great grandmother of David.

VERSE 26

Faith without works is dead – In the same way that the human spirit keeps the body alive, works are the vitalizing "spirit" which keeps one's faith alive. When a believer ceases to act on his faith, that faith becomes a creedal corpse.

So, we see that in context that James 2:14-26 is not teaching the necessity of good works for eternal salvation but that good works are essential for sanctification! We see two types of justification: before God and before men. Paul makes this very distinction in Romans 4:2. He writes, *"For if Abraham was justified by works, he has something to boast about, but not before God."* There is a works justification for the believer, but it is always before men. Abraham's justification in Romans 4 is clearly before God.

The Bible is full of passages that exhort the believer to walk in good works. However, the good works that we do will be judged at the Judgment Seat (Bema) for rewards in the kingdom, not as a test for eternal life. 1 Corinthians 3:12-15 clearly shows the believer's works to be in context of the Judgment Seat (Bema). Paul writes,

> *"Now if any man builds on the foundation with gold, silver, precious stones, wood, hay, straw, each man's work will become evident; for the day will show it because it is to be revealed with fire, and the fire itself will test the quality of each man's work. If any man's work which he has built on it remains, he will receive a reward. If any man's work is burned up, he will suffer loss; but he himself will be saved, yet so as through fire."*

Believers are clearly in view and the loss they may suffer will be loss of reward. Notice that despite of potential loss, they are still saved eternally. The exhortation of this passage is to build on the foundation already laid in Jesus Christ and to do good works that are pleasing to God. It is the motives of the believer's heart that hold the key to hearing "well done" from God. A few verses later in 1 Corinthians 4:5, Paul exhorts, *"Therefore do not go on passing judgment before the time, but wait until the Lord comes who will both bring to light the things hidden in the darkness and disclose the motives of men's hearts; and then each man's praise will come to him from God."* We are told by Paul to examine our own work and to not have a judgmental attitude toward other believers. In Galatians 6:4, he writes, *"But let each one examine his own work, and then he will have reason for boasting in regard to himself alone, and not in regard to another."* Paul illustrates with the principle of sowing and reaping a few verses later in 6:7-10,

> *"Do not be deceived, God is not mocked; for whatever a man sows, this he will also reap. For the one who sows to his own*

flesh will from the flesh reap corruption, but the one who sows to the Spirit will from the Spirit reap eternal life. Let us not lose heart in doing good, for in due time we will reap if we do not grow weary. So then, while we have opportunity, let us do good to all people, and especially to those who are of thehousehold of the faith."

Paul is contextually speaking to believers and poses two possible outcomes. Believers may sow to the flesh and will reap *corruption*, or they may sow to the Spirit and reap *eternal life*. We must remember that eternal life is both a *quantity* of life and a *quality* of life. It is eternal in the sense that it never ends and is the birthright of the believer. All believers have, as a present possession, eternal life. Good works have to do with how we experience the eternal life that we possess. Jesus, in His great intercessory prayer in John 17, says, *"And this is eternal life, that they may know Thee, the only true God, and Jesus Christ whom Thou hast sent."* Experiencing eternal life is linked to how we live our lives in our earthly bodies. Notice the connection in the following verses:

2 Timothy 2:21 – *Therefore, if anyone cleanses himself from these things, he will be a vessel for honor, sanctified, useful to the Master, prepared for every good work.*

2 Thessalonians 2:17 – *Comfort and strengthen your hearts in every good work and deed.*

1 Timothy 6:18 – *Instruct them to do good, to be rich in good works, to be generous and ready to share.*

Hebrews 6:10 – *For God is not unjust so as to forget your work and the love which you have shown toward His name, in having ministered and in still ministering to the saints.*

1 Peter 1:17 – *If you address as Father the One who impartially judges according to each one's work, conduct yourselves in fear during the time of your stay on earth…*

The verses above are just samples of the many times in the Bible that we are exhorted to do good works. It is critical that we understand that good works flow from the heart of a believer who is walking with God. They have absolutely nothing to do with our eternal justification, but they do have great significance in relation to our present walk with God and our future reward for our faithfulness. As we mentioned earlier, these two truths come together beautifully in Ephesians 2:8-9. Our justification is a gift received by grace alone, through faith alone in Christ alone, *"For by grace you have been saved through faith; and that not of yourselves, it is the gift of God…"* But it does not end there. God created us for good works and desires that we walk in them. Verse 10 says, *"For we are His workmanship, created in Christ Jesus for good works, which God prepared beforehand so that we would walk in them."*

We must remember that Free Grace theology promotes good works as the expected response in the life of a believer. However, good works are not guaranteed. They depend on our proper response to the grace of God. Lack of good works cannot change our justified standing before God but will cause us regret at the Judgment Seat of Christ. Our goal should be to hear the words of Jesus in Matthew 25:21, *"…Well done, good and faithful slave. You were faithful with a few things, I will put you in charge of many things; enter into the joy of your master."*

For the grace of God has appeared, bringing salvation to all men, instructing us to deny ungodliness and worldly desires and to live sensibly, righteously and godly in the present age, looking for the blessed hope and the appearing of the glory of our great God and Savior, Christ Jesus, who gave Himself for us to redeem us from every lawless deed, and to purify for Himself a people for His own possession, zealous for good deeds.

Titus 2:11-14

CHAPTER 17:

CONCLUSION

We have laid the foundations for a life filled with grace. I'd like to recap our journey and illustrate by using *The Two Circles* illustration.[1] *The Two Circles* is a visual that helps draw the distinctions between justification truth and sanctification truth. The starting point is our condition without Christ. Nothing I can do will

---

1 For more information on Two Circles Ministries – www.the2circles.org

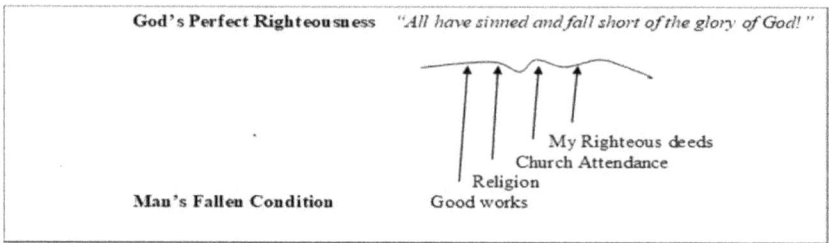

God's Perfect Righteousness   *"All have sinned and fall short of the glory of God!"*

My Righteous deeds
Church Attendance
Religion
Good works

Man's Fallen Condition

ever merit eternal salvation (justification). The very best I can do in my humanity will never be enough to merit God's perfect righteousness. That is why God had to provide the only acceptable solution to our sin problem. That solution was to send His only Son, Jesus, to be the sacrifice for our sins. God loves us so much and demonstrated that love by sending Jesus to the cross as the complete, final sacrifice for sin—all sin—past, present, and future. His resurrection, illustrated by the up arrow on the cross, proved that He was who He said He was and that He did what He said He was going to do. In John 19:39, Jesus said, *"It is finished."* Jesus had finished the work of paying for the sin of the world.

Because of Jesus' death and resurrection, God can now offer eternal life to everyone who will believe in Jesus as the redemptive payment for his or her sin. Believing is not a work we do but is simply receiving the gift that God offers. We must not trust in ourselves, our works, or any other thing or person. We must have faith in Jesus Christ and Him alone!

All sin

100%

Past - Present - Future

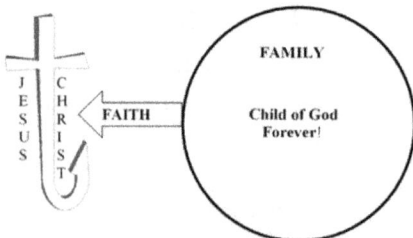

JESUS   CHRIST   FAITH   FAMILY   Child of God Forever!

But as many as received Him, to them He gave the right to become children of God, even to those who believe in His name. (Jn 1:12)

For God so loved the world that He gave His only begotten Son, that whoever believes in Him should not perish, but have eternal life. (Jn 3:16)

When a person believes in Jesus, he or she becomes a member of the family of God. We illustrate this by drawing a large circle which we will call *family*. This is an eternal relationship! Faith must always have an object. It is not how much faith I have, but who the object of my faith is! Jesus, because He is God, is the only One who can save us. He must be the only object of our faith. Once we become His child, He will never cast us out of His family (Jn 10:28-29). Not only are we now children of God, but we also receive other wonderful benefits: we receive the gift of eternal life, God imputes His righteousness to our account, and we are sealed with the Holy Spirit.

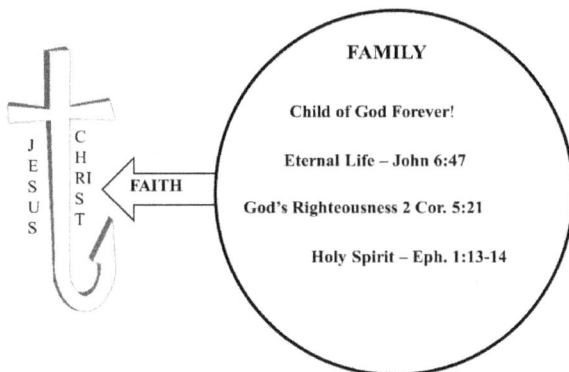

FAMILY

Child of God Forever!

Eternal Life – John 6:47

FAITH

God's Righteousness 2 Cor. 5:21

Holy Spirit – Eph. 1:13-14

JESUS CHRIST

But what about all the commands in the Bible to obey and serve God? If eternal life is truly a gift, then *why not live as I please? What happens when I sin?* This is where the second circle helps us understand the *fellowship* part of our life in the family. Just as a baby grows in a natural family, we have the privilege of growing in God's family. When we are in fellowship with God, we put ourselves in position to grow! We are born into the family by faith alone in Jesus Christ alone. We walk in fellowship as we learn to obey God and faithfully trust His promises.

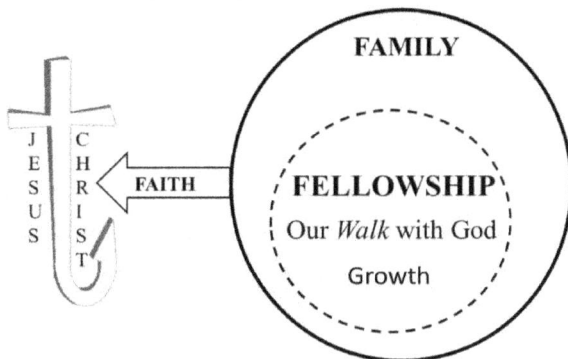

FAMILY

FAITH

FELLOWSHIP

Our *Walk* with God

Growth

JESUS CHRIST

John states clearly in 1 John 1:8, *"If we say that we have no sin, we are deceiving ourselves and the truth is not in us."* This verse is followed by the wonderful promise of 1 John 1:9, *"If we confess our sins, He is faithful and righteous to forgive us our sins and to cleanse us from all unrighteousness."* We would illustrate:

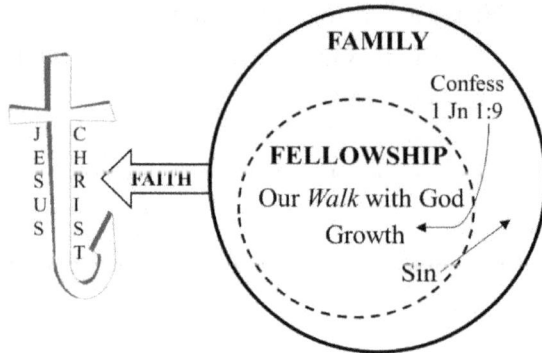

As you can see, sin will hinder our fellowship with God but can never change our eternal status as justified forever. Since Jesus paid for all your sin and offered you eternal life as a free gift, how could sin ever separate you from Him? However, if you continue in sin and do not confess it, you will lose your fellowship with God. The remedy when we become aware of our sin it to confess it and continue to walk in fellowship with God. When we are walking in fellowship with God, we are in the place where we can grow to maturity in Christ. The journey depends on God's grace! Grace that not only saves us for all eternity, but also supplies us with everything we need to live a dependent, productive life. Of course, the ultimate example of grace is the Lord Jesus Christ. As we become more like him, grace will grip our hearts and lead us into a life of humble service. The more like Christ we become, the more gracious we will be.

Julia H. Johnston penned the message of grace wonderfully in her hymn, "Grace Greater Than Our Sin."[2] It is a fitting close to our study!

Marvelous grace of our loving Lord, Grace that exceeds our sin and our guilt! Yonder on Calvary's mount out-poured – There where the blood of the Lamb was spilt. Grace, grace, God's grace, Grace that will pardon and cleanse within; Grace, grace, God's grace, Grace that is greater than all our sin! Sin and despair, like the sea-waves cold, Threaten the soul with infinite loss; Grace that is greater– yes, grace untold – Points to the Refuge, the mighty Cross. Marvelous, infinite, matchless grace, Freely bestowed on all who believe! All who are longing to see His face, Will you this moment His grace receive?

---

2 Julia H. Johnston, *Grace Greater Than Our Sin* (Public Domain, Published in 138 hymnals, 1910).

APPENDIX A

For the reader who wishes to study the topic of unlimited atonement further, the list below of authors and their works will be a good starting place. The list is representative of the different views. It is by no means an exhaustive list. I tend to agree with the first list of authors as I hold the unlimited atonement position and believe that it can be soundly defended from the Bible. Truly, *"The grace of God has appeared, **bringing salvation to all men**."*

Authors that affirm unlimited atonement:

Allen, David L. *The Atonement.* Nashville, Tennessee, B&H Academic, 2019.

Allen, David L. *The Extent of the Atonement; A Historical and Critical Review,* Nashville, Tennessee, B&H Academic, 2016.

Allen, David L. and Steve W. Lemke. *Whosoever Will; A Biblical-Theological Critique of Five Point Calvinism,* Nashville, Tennessee, B&H Academic, 2010.

Anderson, David R. *Free Grace Soteriology.* 3rd ed. The Woodlands, TX: Grace Theology Press, 2015.

Bing, Charles C. *Grace Salvation & Discipleship.* The Woodlands, TX: Texas: Grace Theology Press, 2015.

Bing, Charles C. *Simply by Grace: An Introduction to God's Life-Changing Gift.* Grand Rapids: Kregel Publications, 2009.

Bryson, George. *The Dark Side of Calvinism; The Calvinist Caste System.* Costa Mesa, Calvary Chapel Publishing, 2004

Chay, Fred, and John P. Correia. *The Faith That Saves: The Nature of Faith in the New Testament.* N.p.: Schoettle Publishing Company, 2008.

Craig, William Lane. *The Only Wise God: The Compatibility of Divine Foreknowledge and Human Freedom*. Eugene, OR: Wipf and Stock Publishers, 2000.

Dillow, Joseph. *Final Destiny: The Future Reign of the Servant Kings*. Monument, CO: Paniym Group, 2012.

Eaton, Michael A. *No Condemnation; A Theology of Assurance of Salvation*, Great Briton, Piquant Press, 2011.

Geisler, Norman L. *Chosen But Free: A Balanced View of God's Sovereignty and Free Will*. Minneapolis: Bethany House Publishers, 2010.

Hunt, Dave. *What Love Is This? Calvinism's Misrepresentation of God*. Sisters, OR: Loyal Pub., 2002.

Kerrey, Robert J. *How Does God Draw People To Believe In Jesus?: A Biblical Analysis of Alternative Answers and Why It Matters*. The Woodlands, TX: Grace Theology Press, 2019.

Lightner, Robert P., *The Death Christ Died; A Case For Unlimited Atonement*. Des Plaines, Illinois, Regular Baptist Press, 1967.

Olson, Gordon C. *Beyond Calvinism and Arminianism: An Inductive, Mediate Theology of Salvation*. 3rd ed. Lynchburg, VA: Global Gospel Publishers, 2012.

Olson, Gordon C. *Salvation for All People*, Lynchburg, VA, Global Gospel Press, 2014.

Radmacher, Earl D. *Salvation*. Swindoll Leadership Library. Nashville: Word Pub., 2000.

Ryrie, Charles C. *Basic Theology: A Popular Systematic Guide To Understanding Biblical Truth*. Wheaton: Victor Books, 1986.

Vance, Laurence M. *The Other Side of Calvinism,* Rev. ed. Pensacola, FL: Vance Publications, 1999.

Authors that affirm *limited atonement.*

Berkhof, L. *Systematic Theology.* Grand Rapids: Wm. B. Eerdmans Publishing Co., 1938.

Berkouwer, G. C. *Faith and Justification.* His Studies in Dogmatics. Grand Rapids: W.B. Eerdmans Pub. Co., 1954.

Boettner, Loraine. *The Reformed Doctrine of Predestination.* 7th ed. Grand Rapids: Wm. B. Eerdmans Publishing Co., 1951.

Calvin, John. *Institutes of the Christian Religion.* 2nd ed. John T. McNeill, trans. Ford Lewis Battles, vol. 1, The Library of Christian Classics. Louisville, KY: Westminster John Knox Press, 2011.

MacArthur, John. *The Gospel According to Jesus: What Does Jesus Mean When He Says,"Follow Me"?* 2nd ed. Grand Rapids: Zondervan, 1994.

Packer, J. I. *Concise Theology: A Guide to Historic Christian Beliefs.* Wheaton, IL: Tyndale House, 1993.

Pink, Arthur Walkington. *The Sovereignty of God.* Blacksburg, VA.: Wilder, 2008.

Schreiner, Thomas R., and Ardel B. Caneday. *The Race Set Before Us: A Biblical Theology of Perseverance & Assurance.* Downers Grove, IL: InterVarsity Press, 2001.

Sproul, R. C. *What is Reformed Theology?: Understanding The Basics.* Grand Rapids: Baker Books, 2016.

Steele, David N., and Curtis C. Thomas. *The Five Points of Calvinism: Defined, Defended, Documented,* International Library of Philosophy and Theology: Biblical and Theological Studies. Philadelphia: Presbyterian and Reformed Pub. Co., 1963.

Warfield, B. B. *The Plan of Salvation.* Lexington, KY: Bowker, 201

BIBLIOGRAPHY

Abasciano, Brian J. "Does Regeneration Precede Faith? The use of 1 John 5:1 as a Proof Text." *Evangelical Quarterly* 84, no. 4 (October 2012): 307-322, accessed October 4, 2017, http://search.ebscohost.com/login.aspx?direct=true&db=rlh&AN=82351419&site=ehost-live.

———. "The FACTS of Salvation: A Summary of Arminian Theology/the Biblical Doctrines of Grace." Accessed November 14, 2017, http://evangelicalarminians.org/wp-content/uploads/2013/10/Abasciano.-The-FACTS-of-Salvation1.pdf.

Achtemeier, P.J. Harper & Row, P., & Society of Biblical Literature. 1985. *Harper's Bible dictionary*. 1st ed, Harper & Row: San Francisco.

Allen, David L. *The Atonement: A Biblical, Theological, and Historical Study of the Cross of Christ.* Nashville, B&H Academic, 2019.

———. *The Extent of the Atonement; A Historical and Critical Review.* Nashville, TN, B&H Academic, 2016.

Anderson, David R. *Bewitched: The Rise of Neo-Galatianism.* The Woodlands, TX: Grace Theology Press, 2015.

———. *Free Grace Soteriology.* The Woodlands, TX: Grace Theology Press, 2012.

———. *Position and Condition.* The Woodlands, TX: Grace Theology Press, 2017.

Anderson, David R., and James S. Reitman. *Portraits of Righteousness: Free Grace Sanctification in Romans 5-8.* Lynchburg, VA: Liberty University Press, 2013.

Badger, Anthony B. *Free Grace Theology on Trial.* N.p.: Independent Publishing Platform, 2017.

Baker, Charles F. *A Dispensational Theology.* Grand Rapids: Grace Bible College Publications, 1971.

Barnhouse, Donald Grey. *Teaching the Word of Truth.* Grand Rapids: Wm. B. Eerdmans Publishing Company, 1792.

Bateman, Herbert W., and Gareth L. Cockerill. *Four Views on the Warning Passages in Hebrews.* Grand Rapids: Kregel Publications, 2007.

Bates, Matthew W. *Gospel Allegiance: What Faith in Jesus Misses for Salvation in Christ.* Grand Rapids: Brazos Press, 2019.

———, *Salvation by Allegiance Alone: Rethinking Faith, Works, and the Gospel of Jesus the King.* Grand Rapids: Baker Academic, 2017.

Berkhof, L. *Systematic Theology.* Grand Rapids: Wm. B. Eerdmans Publishing Co., 1938.

Berkouwer, G. C. *Faith and Justification.* His Studies in Dogmatics. Grand Rapids: W.B. Eerdmans Pub. Co., 1954.

Bing, Charles C. *Grace Salvation & Discipleship.* The Woodlands, TX: Texas: Grace Theology Press, 2015.

———. *Simply by Grace: An Introduction to God's Life-Changing Gift.* Grand Rapids: Kregel Publications, 2009.

Boettner, Loraine. *The Reformed Doctrine of Predestination.* 7th ed. Grand Rapids: Wm. B. Eerdmans Publishing Co., 1951.

Cairns, Allen. *Dictionary of Theological Terms.* Greenville, SC: Ambassador Emerald International, 2002.

Calvin, John. *Institutes of the Christian Religion.* 2nd ed. John T. McNeill, trans. Ford Lewis Battles, vol. 1, The Library of Christian Classics. Louisville, KY: Westminster John Knox Press, 2011.

Chafer, Lewis Sperry. *He That Is Spiritual: A Classic Study of the Biblical Doctrine of Spirituality.* Grand Rapids: Zondervan Publishing House, 1975.

_____. *Systematic Theology.* Dallas Seminary Press, 1948.

Chambers, O. 1996, c1947. *Biblical ethics.* Marshall, Morgan & Scott: Hants UK.

Chamblin, Knox "The Law of Moses and The Law of Christ." In *Continuity and Discontinuity: Perspectives on the Relationship Between the Old and New Testaments,* edited by John S. Feinberg, Wheaton: Crossway, 1988.

Chay, Fred. *Legalism is Lethal In the Spiritual Life.* Scottsdale, AR: Grace Line, 2010.

Chay, Fred, and John P. Correia. *The Faith that Saves: The Nature of Faith in the New Testament.* N.p.: Schoettle Publishing Company, 2008.

Chitwood, Arlen L. *Salvation of the Soul: Saving of the Life.* Norman, OK: The Lamp Broadcast, Inc., 2011.

Constable, Tom. *Tom Constable's Expository Notes on the Bible,* 2020 ed. Accessible online at https://planobiblechapel.org/tcon/notes/pdf/galatians.pdf.

Correia, John. *Refreshing Grace: God's Will Our Will In Focus.* Phoenix: Biblical Framework Press, 2012.

Cowan, Christopher W. "The Warning Passages of Hebrews and the New Covenant Community." In *Progressive Covenantalism: Charting a Course Between Dispensational and Covenant Theologies.* Edited by Stephen J. Wellum and Brent E. Parker, 189–213. Nashville: Broadman & Holman, 2016.

Craig, William Lane. *The Only Wise God: The Compatibility of Divine Foreknowledge and Human Freedom.* Eugene, OR: Wipf and Stock Publishers, 2000.

Dieter, Melvin E., et al. *Five Views On Sanctification.* Grand Rapids: Zondervan Pub, 1996.

Dillow, Joseph. *Final Destiny: The Future Reign of the Servant Kings.* Monument, CO: Paniym Group, 2012.

———. "Finding Assurance." In *A Defense of Free Grace Theology: with Respect to Saving Faith, Perseverance, and Assurance.* Edited by Fred Chay, 193–238. The Woodlands, TX: Grace Theology Press, 2017.

———. "Free Grace Has Great Explanatory Power." In *Free Grace Theology: 5 Ways It Magnifies The Gospel,* edited by Grant Hawley, 111–137. Allen, TX: Bold Grace Ministries, 2016.

Ediger, Edwin Aaron. *Faith in Jesus: What Does It Mean to Believe in Him?* Bloomington, IN: West Bow Press, 2012.

Emilio, Ken. "A Theology of Rewards in Heaven." Accessed 03/14/19. http://remnantreport.com/impdf/rewards-01.pdf.

Enns, Paul. *The Moody Handbook of Theology.* Chicago: Moody Press, 1989.

Evans, Tony. *Discover Your Destiny: Let God Use You Like He Made You.* Eugene, OR: Harvest House Publishers, 2013.

Feinberg, Paul D. "Hermeneutics of Discontinuity." In *Continuity and Discontinuity: Perspectives on the Relationship Between the Old and New Testaments, edited by* John S. Feinberg, 109–128. Wheaton: Crossway, 1988.

Flowers, Leighton C. *The Potter's Promise: A Biblical Defense of Traditional Soteriology.* Evansville, IN: Trinity Academic Press, 2017.

Fontecchio, Mark. "Is Repentance Required For Eternal Salvation?" Accessed 03/14/19. https://www.returntotheword.com/Is-Repentance-Required-For-Eternal-Salvation.

Forlines, F. L., and J. M. Pinson. *Classical Arminianism : A Theology of Salvation*. Nashville: Randall House, 2011.

Fuller, Daniel P. *Gospel and Law: Contrast or Continuum?: The Hermeneutics of Dispensationalism and Covenant Theology*. Grand Rapids: William B. Eerdmans Publishing Company, 1980.

Geisler, Norman L. *Chosen But Free: A Balanced View of God's Sovereignty and Free Will*. Minneapolis: Bethany House Publishers, 2010.

Grudem, Wayne. *Free Grace Theology: 5 Ways it Diminishes the Gospel*. Wheaton, IL: Crossway, 2016.

Hawley, Grant. *Dispensationalism and Free Grace: Intimately Linked*. Taos, NM: Dispensational Publishing House, 2017.

Hawley, Grant, and Jeremy Edmondson. *Let the Text Speak: An Introduction to Biblical Hermeneutics*. Allen, TX: Bold Grace Ministries, 2017.

———., ed. *Free Grace Theology: 5 Ways It Magnifies The Gospel*. Allen, TX: Bold Grace Ministries, 2016.

———. *The Guts of Grace*. Allen, TX: Bold Grace Ministries, 2013.

Heiser, Michael S. "Divine Council," ed. John D. Barry et al., *The Lexam Bible Dictionary*. WA: Lexham Press, 2016.

Henshaw, Ben. "The Arminian and Calvinist Ordo Salutis: A Brief comparative Study." Accessed online on 11/14/2017, http://evangelicalarminians.org/the-arminian-and-calvinist-ordo-salutis-a-brief-comparative-study

Hodges, Zane C. "Jesus Is the Propitiation for All, But Only the Mercy Seat for Believers: Romans 3:25 and 1 John 2:2." *Grace in Focus*. (July/August 2006). Accessed November 15, 2019. https://faithalone.org/magazine/y2006/06ja1.html.

———. *The Hungry Inherit: Winning the Wealth of the World to Come.* Chicago: Moody Press, 1973.

———. *Romans: Deliverance From Wrath.* Corinth, TX: Grace Evangelical Society, 2013.

———. "The New Puritanism – Part 3: Michael S. Horton: Holy War with Unholy Weapons." *Journal of the Grace Evangelical Society,* 7. No. 12 (Spring 1994): 17–29.

Horton, Michael. *Introducing Covenant Theology.* Grand Rapids: Baker Books, 2009.

Hunt, Dave. *What Love Is This? Calvinism's Misrepresentation of God.* Sisters, OR: Loyal Pub., 2002.

Johnson, Elliott. *A Dispensational Biblical Theology.* Allen, TX: Bold Grace Academic, 2016.

Kerrey, Robert J. *How Does God Draw People To Believe In Jesus?: A Biblical Analysis of Alternative Answers and Why It Matters.* The Woodlands, TX: Grace Theology Press, 2019.

Luther, Martin. *Commentary on Galatians.* Oak Harbor, WA: Logos Research Systems, Inc., 1997.

MacArthur, John. *The Gospel According to Jesus: What Does Jesus Mean When He Says,"Follow Me"?* 2nd ed. Grand Rapids: Zondervan, 1994.

Mayhue, Richard L. "New Covenant Theology and Futuristic Premillennialism," *The Master's Seminary Journal* 18, no. 2 (September 2007): 221–232.

McClain, Alva J. *Law and Grace.* Winona Lake, IN: BHM Books, 2011.

———. *The Greatness Of The Kingdom.* Winona Lake, IN: BHM Books, 1974.

Merryman, Ronald C. *Galatians: God's Antidote to Legalism*. Colorado Springs: Merryman Ministries, 1999.

———. *Human Volition & Divine Sovereignty*. Colorado Springs: Merryman Ministries, 2016.

_____. *The Believer & The Mosaic Law*. Merryman Ministries, Colorado Springs, Colorado, 2000.

Meyer, Jason C. "The Mosaic Law, Theological Systems, and the Glory of Christ." In *Progressive Covenantalism: Charting a Course between Dispensational and Covenant Theologies*, edited by Stephen J. Wellum and Brent E. Parker, 69–99. Nashville: B&H Academic, 2016.

———. *Lloyd-Jones on the Christian Life: Doctrine and Life as Fuel and Fire*. Wheaton: Crossway, 2018.

Nee, Watchman. *The Salvation of The Soul*. New York: Christian Fellowship Publishers, Inc., 1978.

_____. *Sit, Walk, Stand*. Carol Stream, IL: Tyndale House Publishers, 1977.

Olson, C. Gordon. *Beyond Calvinism and Arminianism: An Inductive, Mediate Theology of Salvation*. 3rd ed. Lynchburg, VA: Global Gospel Publishers, 2012.

_____. *Getting the Gospel Right*. Global Gospel Publishers, Cedar Knolls, New Jersey, 2005.

Oudtshoorn, Andre van. "SOLUS, SOLA: Constructing a Christocentric Faith Model of the 'Ordo Salutis'." *Verbum Et Ecclesia* 35, no.1 (January 2014): 1–9. Accessed October 4, 2017. http://dx.doi.org/10.4102/ve.v35i1.739.

Packer, J. I. *Concise Theology: A Guide to Historic Christian Beliefs*. Wheaton, IL: Tyndale House, 1993.

Panton, D. M. *The Judgment Seat of Christ*. Hayesville, NC: Schoettle Publishing Co., 1984.

Pentecost, J. Dwight. *Things To Come: A Study In Biblical Eschatology*. Grand Rapids: Zondervan, 1964.

Pettegrew, Larry D. "The New Covenant and New Covenant Theology." *The Masters Seminary Journal* 18, no. 2 (September 2007): 181–199.

Peterson, Lorman "Justification," *The Zondervan Pictorial Encyclopedia of the Bible, Volume Three*. Grand Rapids, Michigan, Zondervan Publishing House.

Pink, Arthur Walkington. *The Sovereignty of God*. Blacksburg, VA.: Wilder, 2008.

Radmacher, Earl D. *Salvation*. Swindoll Leadership Library. Nashville: Word Pub., 2000.

———. *What The Church Is All About: A Biblical and Historical Study*. Chicago: Moody Press, 1978.

Reymond, Robert L. "The Traditional Covenantal View." In *Perspectives on Israel and The Church: 4 Views*, edited by Chad O. Brand, 17–68. Nashville: B&H Academic.

Robertson, A. T. *A Grammar of the Greek New Testament in the Light of Historical Research*. Nashville, TN: Broadman Press, 1934.

Ross. Allen P. "The Biblical Method of Salvation: A Case for Discontinuity." In *Continuity and Discontinuity: Perspectives on the Relationship Between the Old and New Testaments*, edited by John S. Feinberg, 161–178. Wheaton: Crossway, 1988.

Ryrie, Charles C. *Balancing The Christian Life*. Chicago: Moody Press, 1972.

———. *Basic Theology: A Popular Systematic Guide To Understanding Biblical Truth*. Wheaton: Victor Books, 1986.

———. *Dispensationalism*. Chicago: Moody Publishing, 2007.

———. *Survey of Bible Doctrine*. Chicago: Moody Publishers, 1972.

———. *The Basis of the Premillennial Faith*. Neptune: Loizeaux Brothers, 1975.

———. "The Necessity of Dispensationalism." *Bibliotheca Sacra* 114, no. 455 (July, 1957): 243–54.

_____. *The Ryrie Study Bible*. Chicago, Moody Press, 1978.

Sapaugh, Gregory. "Is Faith a Gift? A Study of Ephesians 2:8." *Journal of the Grace Evangelical Society,* 7, no. 12 (Spring 1994): 31–43.

Schreiner, Thomas R., and Ardel B. Caneday. *The Race Set Before Us: A Biblical Theology of Perseverance & Assurance*. Downers Grove, IL: InterVarsity Press, 2001.

Seiver, Randy. *Safe And Sound: A Comparative Study of Lordship and "Free Grace" Teaching*. Cartago, Costa Rica: New Wine Press. 2019.

Setran, David P. *Spiritual Formation in Emerging Adulthood: A Practical Theology for College and Young Adult Ministry*. Grand Rapids: Baker Academic, 2013.

Showers, Renald E. *There Really Is A Difference: A Comparison Of Covenant And Dispensational Theology*. Bellmawr, NJ: The Friends of Israel Gospel Ministry, 2002.

Snoeberger, Mark A. "The Logical Priority of Regeneration to Saving Faith in a Theological

Ordo Salutis." *Detroit Baptist Seminary Journal* 7. (September 2002): 49–93. Accessed October 4, 2019. www.dbts.edu/Journal.

Sproul, R. C. *What is Reformed Theology?: Understanding The Basics*. Grand Rapids: Baker Books, 2016.

———. *The Mystery of the Holy Spirit*. Wheaton: Tyndale House Publishers, 1990.

Stanley, Alan P. *Did Jesus Teach Salvation by Works: The Role of Works in Salvation in the Synoptic Gospels*. Eugene, OR: Pickwick Publications, 2006.

Steele, David N., and Curtis C. Thomas. *The Five Points of Calvinism: Defined, Defended, Documented*, International Library of Philosophy and Theology: Biblical and Theological Studies. Philadelphia: Presbyterian and Reformed Pub. Co., 1963.

Strickland, Wayne G. "The Inauguration of the Law of Christ with the Gospel of Christ: A Dispensational View." In *Five Views On Law And Gospel*, edited by Stanley N. Gundry, 229–279. Grand Rapids: Zondervan, 1996.

Strombeck, J. F. *Disciplined By Grace: Studies in Christian Conduct*. 7th ed. Moline: Strombeck Foundation, 1975.

———. *First The Rapture: The Church's Blessed Hope*. Grand Rapids: Kregel Publications, 1992.

———. *Grace and Truth*, 6th ed. Moline: Strombeck Agency, Inc., 1956.

———. *Shall Never Perish*, 9th ed. Moline: Strombeck Foundation, 1964.

———. *So Great Salvation*, 3rd ed. Moline: Strombeck Agency, Inc., 1942.

Tan, Paul Lee. *The Interpretation of Prophecy*. Winona Lake, IN: Assurance Publishers, 1974.

Tenney, Merrill C., *Galatians: The Charter of Christian Liberty*, Wm. B. Eerdmans Pub. Co., Grand Rapids, MI, 1950.

Vance, Laurence M. *The Other Side of Calvinism*, Rev. ed. Pensacola, FL: Vance Publications, 1999.

Vlach, Michael J. "New Covenant Theology Compared With Covenantalism." *The Masters Seminary Journal* 18, no. 1 (Fall 2007): 201–219 .

Wall, Joe L. *Going for the Gold: Reward or Loss at the Judgment Seat of Christ.* The Woodlands, TX: Grace Theology Press, 2015.

Wallace, Daniel B. *Greek Grammar; Beyond the Basics; An Exegetical Syntax of the New Testam*ent. Grand Rapids, Michigan, Zondervan, 1996.

Walvoord, John F. *The Millennial Kingdom.* Grand Rapids: Zondervan, 1959.

Warfield, B. B. *The Plan of Salvation.* Lexington, KY: Bowker, 2017.

Wellum, Stephen J. and Brent E. Parker. *Progressive Covenantalism: Charting a Course Between Dispensational and Covenant Theologies.* Nashville: Broadman & Holman Pub, 2016.

Wemp, Sumner C. *How On Earth Can I Be Spritual?* Thomas Nelson Inc., Publishers, Nashville, New York, 1978.

Wilkin, Robert N. *The Road to Reward: A Biblical Theology of Eternal Rewards.* 2nd ed. Corinth, Texas: Grace Evangelical Society, 2014.

Wilkinson, Bruce, and David Kopp. *A Life God Rewards.* Sisters, OR: Multnomah Publishers, 2002.

William Arndt, Frederick W. Danker, et al., *A Greek-English Lexicon of the New Testament and Other Early Christian Literature.* Chicago: University of Chicago Press, 2000.

Wuest, Kenneth S. *Wuest's Word Studies from the Greek New Testament: For the English Reader.* Grand Rapids: Eerdmans, 1997.

INDEX

www.ingramcontent.com/pod-product-compliance
Lightning Source LLC
Chambersburg PA
CBHW071955090426
42740CB00011B/1957